Did I Take the Wrong Road?

Atara Yuill

In loving memory of my father,
Trevor Yuill.

Prologue

"My mission in life is not merely to survive, but to thrive; and to do so with some passion, some compassion, some humor, and some style."
Maya Angelou

As long as I can remember, I always considered myself to be a writer. My notepad and pen were never kept far away in case I had a strike of inspiration. When I was in school, the paper my mother bought for the new school year in September was usually used up by the end of October. I always had a scribbler on-the-go filled with written bits and pieces. In the last few years, I ditched the paper and pen and switched to a laptop as an attempt to choose a greener alternative. I didn't want to be solely responsible for the global warming effect.

I was always excited at the thought of being the next Nicholas Sparks and I was determined to find similar success in writing. I wanted the book tours and the exclusive interviews on the Ellen DeGeneres show, but my writing career never seemed to succeed. The problem was that I couldn't write much past chapter one. A case of the dreaded writer's block always got the best of me. Sometimes, I didn't feel the emotional connection with the story, and it was impossible to continue writing, or I would get a new idea for a novel that was much more appealing to write. Many times, I questioned my ability to write a novel that would be

DID I TAKE THE WRONG ROAD?

worthy to read. The result of my writing ventures always ended the same: I had many uncompleted projects occupying space on the hard drive of my laptop and no scheduled book tours.

One novel idea I always hoped to explore was in the non-fiction category, a memoir. It's a category I don't read often but one I thought I may write best. As surprising as it may sound, I have a story that I believe is good enough to share.

My idea is to share a story about my imperfect but wonderful family who have had their fair share of struggles but can always count on each other for love and support. I'm aware that people who barely know me, people who know me too well and even complete strangers may read this. My hope is that it will inspire all who read it and also serve the purpose of thanking anyone who has ever helped my family over the years through financial means, kind words, and prayers. The book is also meant as a tribute, a thank you. Your kindness will never be forgotten by my family.

I hope I can convey in my writing just how important each member of my family is and their role in shaping the person I have become. My mother's determination, my father's courage, my brother's kindness, and my sister-in-law's friendship have all played a key role in my life. I know there is no way I can repay them for everything they have done for me over the years. Hallmark just doesn't sell a card that sums it all up, but I thought expressing my gratitude in a novel was a great place to start.

This is not my first attempt at writing a memoir. What stopped me in the past was the vulnerability that I may face if I shared certain aspects of my life. By exposing some of my most inner thoughts and memories, good and bad, I face the possibility of being judged and so does my family. What would people think of us if I shared my family's most private experiences? Would they believe we were crazy? Would they even believe it all happened?

After Dad died in October of 2016, I began to write. It became my way of healing through the most painful experience of my life and let go of some of the sadness I felt. It worked as a therapy of sorts. Writing also helped me preserve memories I hope I will never forget. Even if the book is a major flop, I'll have a guide to read if I get Alzheimer's when I am older.

The more I wrote my story, the more my self-doubts faded. My self-doubts became replaced by pride and confidence as the words poured easily out of me. When I was struggling, my mind kept replaying the wise advice of one of my college classmates. When I was taking the Human Services program, one of my requirements, worth a huge chunk of my grade, was a hundred-page autobiography. It was challenging because as a woman in my early twenties, I had done nothing I deemed noteworthy. I feared my mediocre life would make me fail the project. One of my classmates kept reminding me, "It's your life and you can't screw up your own story."

As you read through the chapter, you may ask yourself, *is this true? Did this really happen?* The short answer to these questions is, yes. The long answer is what you are reading is not the absolute truth. Allow me to explain, I've taken a few psychology classes over the past few years, and one subject I learned about is human memory. Our memories play tricks on us all the time. Our brains encode some of our memories the way we want to remember them whether it is the truth or not. Also, there are many times I forget what I ate for supper last night. For that purpose alone, I would be a fool to promise that this book contains the absolute truth. What I will promise is that it's close to the truth or as much as I can remember of the truth.

Will you find every excruciating detail of my life in this book? Nope. If every moment was written, it wouldn't be a book. It would be an anthology. I had to make the cut somewhere. Some stories are painful and intimate and more important, private. I also must respect that some stories are just not mine to tell.

What I can promise is that every single word was written by me. No ghostwriter did this work. I will not lie and say I didn't wish I had one at times. They may have even written a story from my point-of-view better than what I've written. Sadly, I googled them. Turns out, ghostwriters are expensive. Though, as I stated, I believe writing the book has been some type of therapy for me. Maybe I was meant to write this book all along.

Every grammatical error in this book, sure to make any English professor cringe, is my doing. To make myself sound intelligent, I'll say many of these errors are for creative purposes and not mistakes. They were designed to keep you, the reader, interested and invested in the story. Most writers do it. I was just following their lead.

I also promise I won't ramble on and on and on and on and on and on and on and on and on. Those books are so annoying. See what I did there?

A few of the names have been changed or purposely left out to protect the innocent. Well, actually I'm lying. It's easier to change a few names here and there than it is to learn about privacy and the law.

With all that said, I hope you enjoy the book. I hope it's the best thing you have ever read. In case you don't enjoy the book, it's probably a good time to mention that all sales are final.

Happy Reading,

Atara Yuill

The Beginning of Me

"There are two great days in a person's life – the day we are born and the day we discover why."

William Barclay

I was in the first grade the first time I was invited to go to a friend's house. It wasn't a friend who was a cousin. It wasn't even a friend of my parents who had kids that were roughly my age. The purpose of the visit wasn't to give Mom a break so she could get things done. I was invited to a real friend's house, a girl I went to school with.

Naturally, I had to prepare myself for the special outing. For about a week starting the day I was invited, I had to get myself ready. I tried on Mom's fancy perfume, only used for special occasions, because that was about as special as it got. I put on makeup from a kit I got at Christmas from a great-aunt. My parents did not appreciate the gift as much as I did as they didn't want their six-year-old wearing makeup so the makeup was supposed to be saved for my dolls or, again, one of those extremely special occasions. The event of going to a new friend's house when I had never been to a friend's house before, definitely called for makeup. I applied the lipstick and the blush. No six-year-old is probably good at putting on makeup, and I was no exception. I am not even great at putting on makeup now. The blush on my cheeks made Mom think I had a rash, which she probably figured was from the new soap. I didn't tell her the difference, and for years we avoided that brand of soap because of my allergy.

Finally, the day was drawing near. I practiced playing board games and throwing around a baseball with my brother. I tried to remember all the funny jokes I knew. I listened to my brother's stories about what he did when he went to his friends' houses. Needless to say, I was excited to go.

I had a great time at her house. We played outside and played with her dolls. We watched television. In fact, I was maybe just a tad jealous of her cable television because our television only had three channels and one channel was French. Her thirty-six channels were unimaginable to me back then.

While I was at her house, her father assembled her new bed that had been ordered straight from the catalog. Her grandmother came to visit and brought us cookies. My friend and I sat down and enjoyed a cookie and a glass of milk.

As young as six-years-old, I knew her family differed greatly from my own. They were *The Keatons* from *Family Ties* and my family compared more to *The Simpsons*. Sure, my family loved each other, but things had a habit of not working out the way they were supposed to in our lives. Everything seemed to work out in her family.

As hectic as life could get, I knew I could always count on my family and the love we shared. Oddly enough, if you asked my mother if she loved my father the day she married him, she would say 'no'. She enjoyed spending time with him, and she felt safe with him. She knew she didn't want him to be with anyone else and that she didn't want to be with anyone else. But she doesn't believe she loved him when they married. She thought they had the potential to fall in love. Her belief was maybe love is not always 'true' love right away, like in the fairy tales. Sometimes, maybe love – true love – is a deep-rooted emotion that grows over time. It takes years to discover the qualities and quirks of that person. Even in our old age, we are constantly evolving, and we still find new things we love about our significant other.

Mom could be wrong about her theory of love but she's probably right about one thing, she didn't love Dad when she married him. She didn't have time to realize if she loved him or not. They married shortly after they started to date.

Mom and Dad met at a party in September. Mom didn't want to go to the party. She worked that day, and she was tired. She was also afraid that she wouldn't know too many people but her friend wanted her to go, so she reluctantly agreed.

Just like Mom expected, she felt a little awkward at the party. Her friend was dating someone, and she felt like a third wheel. She saw Dad by the door when she was leaving to have a cigarette. He opened the door for her and commented on her beautiful eyes. Mom always felt self-conscious about her eyes and appreciated the comment. She was the only one out of her four siblings that had brown eyes. They all had blue eyes like their mother, and she envied them.

When Mom came back in, Dad was waiting to talk to her. They talked a lot that night and Mom thought she felt a connection she never quite felt with anybody else.

Mom and Dad only lived thirty minutes; give or take, from each other for most of their lives. Mom was one of the last classes that graduated from Tignish Regional High School. Dad went to trade school in Summerside for mechanics, an hour away from Mom's school. Mom was also three years older than Dad.

Before the party, they knew 'of' each other. West Prince was too small not to. Dad's family sold tractors and Mom's family were farmers. Their families had conducted business together a few times in the past. My paternal grandfather even had supper a few times at my maternal grandparents' house. Yet Mom and Dad never spoke before the party.

Their instant bond was unlike any other either had ever experienced. Dad proposed on Valentine's Day. It was less than six months after they started to date. Mom hadn't even met Dad's family yet, but it felt like the right move for them.

Dad hid the ring in a vest that his mother made for Mom. Mom agreed to marry him, but she wanted a long proposal and they originally planned to get married in two years. After much debate, they decided that they might enjoy a wedding before Christmas that same year. After another discussion, the date changed to August 24th, 1985. It was the same year they got engaged – only seven months after my father proposed.

Dad had decided to become a Catholic before they married. He was Anglican, but he was non-practicing.

He could see how important religion was to Mom and if he planned to start a family with her, then he wanted to be part of the same religion. Dad believed this was also an important step in gaining the approval he desperately wanted from Mom's family. He respected the Catholic religion and had friends who were Catholic. When he was younger, he had gone to mass with them a few times and had really enjoyed it. A lot of the beliefs of the Catholic religion and the Anglican religion were similar.

From the stories and pictures, I gathered from their wedding, it was beautiful. Their new life together began with their friends and family by their side. They had no regrets and wanted to start their family immediately. Mom became pregnant with Landon only three months after their wedding.

Nearly five years after Landon was born when Mom found out she was pregnant with me, she cried. Most women cry tears of joy or squeal with delight when they find out they are pregnant. But it wasn't the case with my mother. My mother wailed in sadness. She didn't cry because she hated children. She didn't get upset because she was vain and worried that a baby would wreck her womanly figure. It was the timing. The timing couldn't have been worse to have a baby.

Her husband was in a hospital in Ontario. They already had a four-year-old son that depleted her daily energy. And, did I mention she was technically homeless? Their house went up in flames a few months before. The construction on the house, and the insurance money to pay for the house, was slow.

Mom finally had no choice but to accept her pregnancy. Her weeks of lamenting, 'Why God?', or hoping Aunt Flo was just a little late, were over. She finally embraced the pregnancy and allowed herself to believe a baby would bring joy and laughter into a family needing desperately to find a little joy. She hoped she would have a little girl to complete her family.

The rest of the family had a hard time accepting the news. My paternal grandmother claimed stress could do some strange things to a woman's body. She believed that my mother was just stressed, not pregnant. Mom's jeans, which could no longer fasten, and the weird cravings she was experiencing begged to differ that it was 'only stress'.

My maternal grandmother had an even stranger reaction. "I'm thrilled for you, but I had hoped that your older sister would be the one who would become pregnant next."

It turns out my maternal grandmother got her wish because my aunt was indeed pregnant. My cousin and I were born only three days apart, me being older.

Even her family doctor shook his head in disbelief. Mom had such a rotten labor with my brother that he probably hoped she wouldn't be crazy enough to tempt fate again. She had the measles during her first pregnancy. The old wives' tales of babies born without arms or legs got the best of her, and she lived in fear most of the pregnancy. Three long days were spent in labor before the baby became distressed and they had to do a caesarian section which led to my brother needing an IV in his head. Half of his head needed to be shaved and Mom vowed she would not take his picture until he got a little cuter.

Because of all the medications that Dad was taking and the procedures he had done since his accident, it was questioned if he could have children. No test was ever done to confirm or deny their beliefs. It was more of a 'let's wait and see' game they were playing.

Essentially, with all the above information presented, I am their miracle sent from heaven, kind of like a surprise on Christmas Day. You know when you were little or, okay I'll admit it—I still write to Santa, but you open a gift which wasn't on your list, and it turns out that the surprise gift is your favorite gift. It's better than anything you could ever ask for.

Mom's pregnancy with me was a period of transitions and not just because she would soon have to start waking up in the middle of the night again to feed a crying baby. Landon was almost five and had long stopped waking in the middle of the night. Mom's pregnancy was challenging because the house was being built, Landon would soon start school, and Dad's health was still a major concern. To make matters worse, my great-grandmother had also passed away during this time.

∞

The new house was coming together quickly. The mouse-infested house was built in plenty of time before I was born. Yes, I said mouse-infested house. Most people would think a new house, never lived in before, would be the cat's meow. What they don't tell you is how many little varmints get in when the walls are being constructed. It's very logical when you think of it. It's easy for mice to get in when there are no walls and no roof.

Imagine my father trying to impress his grandfather with a tour of his new house. When it was time to leave, my great-grandfather put his coat on and felt something moving in his pocket. When my great-grandfather reached in, he pulled out two mice. Guess what the funny story for the next decade was—at every family get-together?

∞

I'm told my great-grandmother was an eccentric lady. You had no choice but to love her. Granny wore mismatched clothing and could knit just about anything. She was creative, kind, and funny.

Granny was a little old-fashioned in some of her beliefs; like banking. She didn't believe in banking at a proper bank. Granny stored her money in her own unique way. She hid money all over the house; under beds, in dressers, and in compartments in the fridge and freezer. You never knew where you would find money and it was a daunting task after she died.

Shortly after Mom and Dad married, they went for a visit to Granny and Grampy's house. Mom had met them before when she was engaged to Dad. Because they had such a short engagement, she didn't have time to really get acquainted with them. It was important for her to get to know them because Dad loved them a great deal.

The morning Mom woke up in their guest bedroom, she made the bed. As she was tucking some of the sheets and blankets under the mattress, a fold of money fell out. There was more than just a few dollars in the fold. A lot of money was there, hundreds of dollars.

"Let's get out of here," Mom told Dad. She spoke with the same sound of urgency that might have been used if she had witnessed a murder.

Dad explained it was their way of living, but Mom was convinced that they were testing her. She worried they may have miscounted money or money would go missing and they would blame her. Mom tried carefully not to make any more discoveries for the rest of her visit.

Granny didn't believe in throwing things out either. She thought most things always had a second use and didn't just belong in a landfill. After Dad had the surgery to put the feeding tube in, Granny was determined to find another use for the bags that held the formula. She had bags spread out all over her kitchen by her plants. She was convinced they would be great to water the plants, but she couldn't figure out how to get the water to stop falling through the tubing.

As Mom got to know them, she really grew to appreciate and love them as if they were her own grandparents. She wasn't very old when all her grandparents died and the concept of grandparents was foreign to her until she became a part of Dad's family.

Eventually, ready or not to have a baby, nine months were up, and Mom went into labor in early May. They dropped Landon off at a family member's house and drove to the hospital in Summerside.

Although I have never made the trip from Tignish to Summerside pregnant, I can imagine the hour-long car ride would be difficult. On Prince Edward Island, the number of potholes was only half the battle.

My father has always been efficient behind the wheel. He could get you where you wanted to be in a hurry, but he could not avoid construction.

There was a detour that day, and it was going to take time. Dad didn't want to take the chance of having to deliver a baby on the side of the road.

"I have to get through. My wife's having a baby," Dad told the construction workers.

The workers let him go through the site. Mom winced as they drove over the bumps and maneuvered through the cones but they would soon be at the hospital.

She spent over thirty hours in labor. There was a lot of screaming involved during those thirty hours. She blamed Dad for putting her in that condition, and she made the vow she would never ever get pregnant again. But as hard as she tried, she was not progressing any further with the dilation. The nurses and doctor finally decided the only way I was coming into the world was by a caesarian section.

"I think we could have taken the detour," Dad told her before she went into surgery. "Heck, we could have gone on a tour of the whole island."

The surgery seemed like a great opportunity to take care of all the business and stop anything like this from happening to her body again. My father was too scared to contradict Mom, but his mother wasn't. Nena followed the surgeon around and made him promise he would not tie her tubes. Now was not the time to be letting Mom decide life-altering decisions.

On May 4th, 1991, I was born. I would have stayed in her womb if it hadn't been for the surgeon forcibly removing me.

My father excitedly told Mom, "You did it, Lorna. We have a boy, and now we have a girl. You did great."

My mother was coming out of anesthesia. She was tired and drowsy. She didn't care if she gave birth to a girl or an elephant.

Mom insisted that I was a beautiful baby. According to her, I was television-show worthy. I didn't have a cone-shaped head, my hair was perfect, and I was proportionate. I'm a little reluctant to believe her because, like Landon, the only baby pictures that were ever taken of me was when I was near one-years-old.

Landon loved me before he even met me. He was so excited to meet me that the day after I was born, while Dad was sleeping on the couch, Landon decided that they both needed haircuts to impress me. He first cut his own hair unevenly and then made a few cuts in Dad's hair before Dad woke up. Mom wasn't excited or impressed with the new haircuts that Dad hid with baseball hats.

A few days after they came home, Mom started to get intense stomach pain. She tried to ignore it. She just had surgery. The pain was to be expected but she eventually had to go to outpatients.

"You're having a gallbladder attack," the doctor explained to her. "We need to take it out. You need to have surgery."

"I have a newborn baby. Is there anything we can do to avoid surgery right now? Are there any medications I can take?"

"I'm afraid not," he explained.

Landon and I went to Nena and Papa's house, for an unplanned visit while Dad brought Mom to the hospital.

That evening, a little after supper, when Dad was on his way home from the hospital, he decided he wanted to bring us home. He thought we should sleep in our own beds.

Nena didn't want Dad to bring us home. According to Nena, Dad would have to go back to the hospital in the morning, and I was already asleep. She also had concerns that Dad wasn't healthy enough to look after us on his own, especially since I was a newborn. A baby needed a woman, in Nena's opinion.

"She's my baby," Dad tried to argue.

"You can't take the kids," Nena replied.

"Fine," he finally said. "But I'm coming to get the kids tomorrow to bring them home," Dad warned before he reluctantly went home.

That night, in the middle of the night, when everyone was asleep, Dad used his key to get into Nena and Papa's house. He quietly went into the room where I was sleeping. He took me and then he got Landon.

When Nena went to give me my milk, she soon discovered what took place. Needless to say, she wasn't pleased with Dad.

The next morning, she drove to our house in Tignish. She knocked on our door, but Dad wouldn't answer. She didn't have a house key, so Dad won the battle.

Mom had just gotten home from the hospital and Dad started to have pain. It was exactly like Mom described her pain.

"It must be sympathy pain," someone told him. "It's just in your head."

The pain wasn't going away though. He went to the doctor's office and discovered he was also having a gallbladder attack. He needed to have surgery too.

By the time that Mom and Dad were both recovered, it was already June. Only the basics in house cleaning had been done and the yard desperately needed to be cut. More importantly, I still hadn't been baptized.

Had it been up to my maternal grandmother, I would have been baptized almost immediately after I was born. She tried not to voice her opinion about the importance of baptism, but Mom knew how important it was. As soon as she and Dad felt better, my baptism was planned.

"Thank God, Lorna," Mémé joked. "I thought you were going to wait until she could walk to church herself."

Dad

"A person who falls and gets back up is much stronger than a person who never fell."

Unknown

Dad had been hurt in a work accident only four years before I was born. He was working to gain experience he needed so he could obtain his heavy equipment mechanics license. It was just before his morning coffee break, and he was finishing his work up and filled a tire with air. The tire blew, and the rim hit him in the face and knocked him back into a brick wall. The pressure was so intense that the outline of his body was visible on the brick wall.

The immediate effects of the accident made him very hyper, and his head pounded. In the ambulance, he couldn't lie down. He was too afraid that he would pass out. His body was in fight-or-flight mode, and he was running on adrenaline.

He was given the choice when they reached the highway near Tyne Valley whether he wanted to go to the hospital in O'Leary or Summerside. He chose O'Leary. It was closer to home, and he wasn't sure how badly he was hurt. The ambulance driver didn't expect that he would be kept in O'Leary long. He stayed in the parking lot and left the ambulance running because he thought they would be going to a bigger hospital shortly. The doctor on call, in the outpatient department, surprised them all by keeping Dad in the hospital in O'Leary.

By that evening at supper time, they were still learning about some of the issues resulting from the accident. His nose was broken. He couldn't keep anything down that he ate. As time passed, nausea and vomiting became the norm. It was an everyday occurrence. He also got migraines which just would not go away, even with pain medication.

The doctors on PEI sent him to the hospital in Moncton, New Brunswick for more testing. They wanted to find out why he was experiencing so much vomiting and migraines. Some of the tests they did in Moncton revealed that his skull had broken. In addition, to his broken skull, significant damage had been done to his sinus cavity. Some of the doctors who examined him believed the vomiting was due to the damaged message pathway from the stomach to the brain. The best way one doctor could explain Dad's injuries was by making the comparison that the brain is like a bowl of jelly. Once it's shaken, it can never be the same again.

∞

After Dad's accident, he wasn't able to return to work. He was too sick. He had an insurance claim, and they were paying for his loss of wages, medications, and any other expenses that were occurring.

About three years after they began to pay him, the insurance started to insinuate Dad's injuries weren't a direct result of the accident. They insisted it was more of a coincidence than anything that Dad started to experience poor health after the accident. They believed he might have gotten sick even if he hadn't gotten hurt at work. According to them, it wasn't a work-related sickness, and they would not be responsible to pay for his claim anymore.

My parents were devastated and scared to lose his benefits. They did their best to convince them they were wrong.

"I don't understand," Mom said at one of their meetings, "Trevor went to work that morning. He was fine. He didn't have any health problems. He didn't come home the same way and he hasn't been the same since that day. Tell me, how is this not a work-related accident?"

"Mrs. Yuill," the representative for the insurance, said quietly, "I can definitely understand your frustration, but we had a doctor examine Trevor and review his file. He does not see a direct link between the accident and Trevor's health."

She took a deep breath when they were on their way home.

"Imagine that Trevor, they found a doctor who will say what they want him to. Do you think that doctor will earn his bonus this year?"

Dad wrinkled his nose in disgust, "What are we going to do?"

Mom bit her lip before replying, "We're going to fight it as hard as we can."

Mom and Dad got letters from their family doctor supporting their claim. They asked for letters from most of the doctors who had consulted in Dad's care since the accident. Most of them didn't want to get involved. There would be a lot of paperwork involved, and they didn't have the time. They would also lose time from their practice if it ever went to court.

For every ounce of support that Mom and Dad gained to prove their claim that the accident was the catalyst, the start of his poor health, insurance went above and beyond to prove them wrong. Most of the time at the meetings, their ideas seemed absolutely ridiculous to Mom and Dad. It was hard to believe what they were hearing.

"We believe it's psychological," they were told.

"You think I want to be sick?" Dad asked. "This isn't a life I want to live. I wanted to work. I had a business that was going to be mine. This was not part of the plan."

"Nevertheless," one representative said, as he wrote notes in his file, "you should be tested by a mental health professional."

"Okay," Dad replied. He knew if he refused the psych consult, they wouldn't do anything more for him.

He was admitted for the evaluation. During his admission, his IQ was tested, along with various other psychological tests. He met with several psychologists and psychiatrists who interrogated him. They also met with Mom and they questioned her alone and then met with Dad and questioned him alone. They felt as if they were criminals in a conspiracy together.

"Do you think you have a mental illness?" one specialist asked Dad point-blank.

Dad took a minute to collect his thoughts. "Isn't it your job to tell me if you think I have a mental illness?"

"If you can give an answer like that," the specialist said, with a small smile on his face, "then there isn't much sense for you to be here."

Dad was discharged after that. Mentally, he was fine. They couldn't blame his health on a psychological illness, but insurance was still refusing to cover any more of his expenses.

Many more meetings later, a decision was finally reached.

"You need to go back to school and retrain for a new career if you can't be a mechanic anymore."

Dad was feeling miserable at that time.

"I'm not sure if I can even tolerate going to school right now."

"If you don't, you will lose your benefits."

Once again, Mom and Dad tried to find a solution. They asked their family doctor to compose a letter to persuade the insurance company that Dad was in no shape to be going to school, but their efforts were to no avail. If he didn't go to school, he would lose any compensation he was getting.

He started his business course in 1990, the year before I was born. If he couldn't be a mechanic, he would at least gain experience in running a business and still may be able to take over his father's business in a different capacity.

He started having problems with his pancreas when he was in school. His pancreas was inflamed. He had pancreatitis and was in a lot of pain. He ended up in the hospital a lot. He spent most of his time rocking back and forth, trying to ease the intense pain.

One doctor compared Dad's health issues to problems a person with an eating disorder would face. He had lost nearly seventy pounds since he had gotten hurt. Dad just didn't have the psychological issues that were associated with eating disorders. He was losing too much weight, and his body had to work hard to keep everything going. Although it isn't well understood, pancreatitis can be an effect of an eating disorder.

Abdominal trauma can also be another factor associated with pancreatitis. When the accident happened, he was pushed back towards the wall. The tire hit his skull, and it also hit his stomach.

Eventually, they had to remove half of Dad's pancreas. They often try not to do surgery on the pancreas unless it is absolutely necessary because the pancreas can easily be damaged. It is also considered to be a complicated and high-risk surgery. When it came to Dad, there wasn't any other choice because he kept having attacks.

About a year or so after I was born, Dad had his surgery. A partial pancreatectomy is the proper medical term for his surgery. Neither Mom nor Dad realized how big of a surgery it was at the time, especially without the technology available for healthcare that they have today.

One of the complications from the surgery was that Dad became a diabetic. He was a brittle one at that. He needed to constantly monitor his blood sugar levels and his formula for his feeding tube needed to be changed because the initial formula contained too much sugar. He required four doses of insulin daily.

He had flunked out of his course because he had missed so much time. The insurance was still refusing to believe it was all caused by his accident and they stopped his benefits.

Mom and Dad met with politicians. Sometimes because they were so emotional, Dad's parents went with them. They needed more people to hear the conversation and my grandparents were actively involved in politics and knew many of the politicians.

"It's not really a political thing," one politician said. "There is nothing I can do."

My grandmother got so upset at one meeting because it seemed nobody could help them. She had to leave because she was about to lose her temper—and no one wants to see a redhead lose their temper. The office was tiny, and she couldn't get out, so she crawled underneath the table to get out.

Mom and Dad met with lawyers. They wanted to fight it. It wasn't fair because the accident caused everything. He was working the day of the accident. Now he couldn't work.

Lawyers were willing to take the case, but they never promised they could win. Some also required a hefty retainer, one Mom and Dad couldn't afford. Especially when Dad wasn't getting any kind of salary.

One night after another unsuccessful meeting, Dad looked at Mom. He was discouraged.

"What are we going to do, Lorna? It's hopeless. Whatever we do, they just do it better. I can't afford the team of lawyers they have. We find a doctor, and they get one of their own specialists to say something else."

Mom reached for Dad's hand.

"I think we have to let it go. We can't afford to keep fighting, and you don't have the stamina to keep fighting with them right now. We need to worry about your health."

"It's not fair," Dad sighed.

"You're right!" Mom agreed. "But for your sanity and my own, we have to let it go. We have to move on with our lives. We have two kids to think about."

"This isn't right," Dad said, quietly.

"We'll be okay," Mom promised.

When they gave up their pursuit, they were happier. It was the most peace they had felt since they had started to bicker with the insurance company. They no longer felt like criminals, trying to pull an insurance scam. They never worried if they were going to be cut off or what the insurance company would ask them to do next. They could concentrate on Dad's health.

As peaceful as they felt, they were still furious with the situation. Dad qualified to receive a disability allowance, but it wasn't enough money. Dad had too many appointments and needed a lot of medications.

They started to worry about money. Mom would have to carefully budget every cent they had, and still, sometimes it wasn't enough. We wouldn't have gotten through without help from friends and family.

A Christmas to Remember

"Hardships often prepare ordinary people for an extraordinary destiny."

C. S. Lewis

Despite Dad's health, their finances, or any other concerns, Mom always made Christmas the highlight of the year for the Yuill family. She went above and beyond trying to make each Christmas unique and special. The house was always decorated with a scene that was worthy of any holiday movie. Our tree would always have an abundance of gifts underneath the tree, bought with change and bottle money that was saved all year. The cupboards and fridge would be stocked with enough food to last a long time, in case it stormed for a month.

∞

During my first Christmas, our house was beautifully decorated, the groceries were bought, the meat pies and sweets were already baked, and the shopping was done. It was supposed to be a perfect Christmas but Dad's health was threatening Mom's plans.

It was Christmas Eve and the sun was starting to set. Snow was softly falling but as beautiful as the winter scene outside was, Mom couldn't enjoy it. She was in the hospital visiting Dad.

Her eyes were focused on Dad. Dad was lying in the hospital bed because he was having a pancreas attack. He was in a lot of pain and was attempting to find a position that would allow him a reprieve from the pain.

The attack had started a few days before. Mom hoped and prayed that the IV medications, that Dad had been prescribed immediately following his admission, would work quickly and he would be able to go home before Christmas. Despair was setting in because she knew, in truth, that he would not be coming home for Christmas.

"Go home with the kids," Dad told her. "It's getting dark and I'm not much company."

Mom gave him a hug, "Next year will be different. You'll be home with us."

Mom drove cautiously to her sister's house. It was dark by that point and the snow was still falling. The roads were becoming slippery and Mom feared her summer tires just weren't prepared for the snow.

She wanted to go home. She didn't feel like visiting with anyone but it was her last chance to deliver gifts before Christmas morning so she stayed her course as Landon and I sat in the backseat.

∞

"We can't stay long," Mom warned Landon as she unbuckled me from my car seat.

"Okay," Landon agreed.

Christmas carols quietly hummed from the radio, the house was toasty warm, and delicious smells were coming from the oven. It was difficult for Mom not to feel a twinge of jealousy. That's how she envisioned spending my first Christmas, but it wasn't going to happen.

"You should stay," Mémé suggested.

Mom smiled.

"I can't. It's Christmas and Landon and Atara's gifts are home. It wouldn't be fair."

The falling snow was beginning to form drifts. The wind howled and Mom silently cursed that she hadn't changed the tires on the car in time for winter.

∞

After a short time, we left. The laneway leading to our house was covered in a thick blanket of snow. With a small prayer and her foot on the pedal, she turned in the laneway, hoping she wouldn't get stuck. With a stroke of luck, she managed to get the car in the laneway just far enough that it would be safe from any damage that the plow could do.

"I want to go to bed," Landon said.

Mom glanced at the clock. It was his usual bedtime.

"You can stay up!"

"No," Landon replied, "I'm ready for bed."

She tucked her five-year-old son into bed. She had hoped Landon might want to stay up so she wouldn't be alone on Christmas Eve. The risk of Santa not coming if he was awake made Landon determined that he was going to go to bed on time and she was left to spend the evening by herself.

For nearly three hours, she assembled toys that she knew would likely end up in the garbage sometime in January as she sipped on a glass of wine. A small tear started to fall from her eye as she reflected on that year's circumstances. She stubbornly wiped it away.

"Tomorrow will be better," she told herself.

∞

The next morning, she awoke early to Landon's demands to see what Santa brought. Determined to make it a better day, she put a smile on her face and eagerly got out of bed.

The phone started to ring.

"Hello?" Mom answered.

"I'm getting a pass for a few hours," Dad shared. "Can you come and get me?"

"Sure," Mom said, "we'll be there as soon as we can."

As quick as she could get two kids and herself ready, we were out the door. What Mom didn't expect was to get stuck. She didn't have to shovel for long before a neighbor came to help.

"I'm trying to go and get Trevor," she explained.

"Let me go and get him," he offered.

"Are you sure?" Mom asked, not wanting to keep him from his family.

"Yes," he stated, "it's my Christmas present to you. Go back inside with the kids and get warmed up."

Mom continued to shovel. It would give her something to do while she waited for Dad to get home.

∞

"You have to take me back to the hospital," Dad said.

Dad had only been home for an hour when the pain quickly crept back. He was in agony.

"Are you sure you can't stay any longer?" Mom asked. She had just gotten the meal ready and she wanted all of us to eat together.

"I wish I could," Dad grimaced. "I'm going out of my mind with the pain."

"Okay," Mom uttered as she started to get Landon and me ready to go again.

"Trevor," Mom said, as she drove near the hospital entrance, "I won't be able to go inside with you. The kids need to get home."

"Okay," Dad said, as he got out. "I'm really sorry this is happening."

That evening, as Landon played with his toys and I napped, Mom started to clean up. It dawned on her that she hadn't seen the dog all day.

"Gypsy?" Mom called out.

The dog was nowhere in sight. She started to search for him.

"Where is he?" Landon asked.

"I'm not sure," Mom said. "I'll check the basement."

When Mom went down to the basement, her heart instantly clutched inside her chest. Our beloved dog was dead. Gypsy was the dog my parents rescued from the shelter just before they married. It was the first thing Mom and Dad vowed to take care of and he was gone.

Mom came back upstairs. She tried to stop the tears from falling from her eyes. It was important that Landon got to enjoy the rest of his Christmas. She would find a way to tell him about Gypsy tomorrow.

Landon couldn't help but notice something was wrong. He wanted to find a way to make Mom feel better.

"I have good news, Mom."

"What good news is that?" Mom asked.

"You can take back that doll that's underneath your bed because Santa brought Atara the very same doll."

Daddy's Girl

"It was my father who taught me to value myself."

Dawn French

From the moment I was born, I had a special and instant bond with my father. Dad was always disappointed with the important milestones he missed with Landon. Landon was only six months old when Dad got hurt and because Dad was in the hospital so much when Landon was young, he missed a lot of the important steps. I was the second chance for Dad to get to experience it all.

Landon had to go to school and Mom worked. It was just Dad and me. Wherever he went, I followed. I was his shadow. I never found myself too far away from him, and when I was, I found it difficult. I didn't know what to do with myself.

I often went to appointments with Dad. There was usually no other place for me to go and I would have been devastated if he wouldn't have taken me. Dad never had a problem taking me.

One appointment he had was in Halifax, Nova Scotia. We didn't have the convenience of being able to leave PEI when we wanted to. Dad and I had to follow the ferry schedule because the Confederation Bridge was not built yet. We often left the night before and stayed at Dad's brother's house in Truro, an hour out of Halifax.

Naturally the day of his appointment, I thought I was going with him. I didn't realize that Dad had no intentions of taking me to the appointment and he left before I woke up.

When I woke up and realized he left me behind, I was angry. *He thinks he can do that to me. Leave me behind with these people I don't know very well. Well, I'll show him. Let's see what he thinks when I don't talk to him anymore.*

The entire day I vowed I would not talk to him when he got back. I was far too angry, and he would pay the price. When he came back to my uncle's in the afternoon, I changed my mind.

I quickly ran to him and hugged him.

"Dad, Dad!" I said, breaking my vow of silence, "I missed you so much."

My silence didn't last very long. I was too excited that he came back and I forgot I was mad.

∞

A lot of my early memories involve the hospital. It seems it was where we spent the most time. Every second day, Dad drove Mom to work in Alberton and we went to the hospital in O'Leary.

When we got to the hospital, Dad and I would go to the family room. The nurse would hook him up to his machine so he could have his nutrition go through his feeding tube and we'd wait for most of the day for the formula to enter his body. When the formula was finished entering Dad's body, it would be time to pick Mom up from work.

I liked going to the hospital most days. They had more television channels to choose from and most times I got to decide what to watch. It was usually only Dad and me in the family room.

Besides the great television, there was almost always something interesting happening at the hospital. The nurses who came in to check on Dad were friendly. Some even had a joke or two to tell. Some of the older patients would come in and give me their undivided attention. Other days, Nena would pay Dad and me a visit.

I don't remember when we stopped going to the hospital, but before I started school, the trips to the hospital stopped. He had his own machine to take his feeding at home.

The way he set up his schedule for his tube feeding meant that I was on my own for the mornings. He would only finish around noon. Sometimes I would lay in Mom and Dad's room until the feeding was done. Often, I was bored and needed to move around. It was too constricting in the bedroom.

I learned how to become highly self-efficient when I was young. While Dad was still connected to the machine, I made myself breakfast. I only liked the cereal with the raisins. The raisins were also the only thing I ate, and the dog ate the rest of the cereal. We made the perfect team. After breakfast, I made a fort. It wasn't so much of a fort as a blanket thrown over the coffee table, but it still did the trick. Inside the fort, I would play with my dolls or play with Landon's toys, especially the ones he wouldn't usually let me play with when he was home.

When Dad's feeding finished, he would make my lunch. If he was having a good day, he would often try to find an activity for us to do that I would enjoy. In the winter, we went for drives on the ski-doo. When the weather was nice, and the snow was gone, we would go for drives on the bicycle. He taught me the alphabet and how to count. Sometimes Dad would help someone with a tractor, and I went with him.

When Dad was having a bad day, it would be quiet. He often felt too miserable on those days to do much else but lift his head. Usually, these were the days we would watch movies. I would play with my toys while he rested on the couch. Sometimes I had to relent and play with my toys in his bedroom. On these days, I brought him things, and he would make me crackers and cheese for lunch. Sometimes Dad would feel miserable for more than a few days and wind up in the hospital. Mom would have to find a sitter or rely on family members to watch me until Dad was feeling better.

Before I started school, I recall there were many times that Dad was admitted to the hospital. Sometimes it would only be in Summerside but often it would be further away. Dad hated being in the hospital. He felt it was a form of imprisonment and he usually only went to the hospital when he had no other choice. When he went to the hospital, he would be incredibly ill and weak. The admission time probably lengthened significantly because he waited so long to go to the hospital.

It was challenging when Dad was admitted to the hospital. All our daily routines changed. If he was sick unexpectedly, Mom had to find a place I could go when she went to work. Mom had to work, make the meals, try to keep up with everything around the house, and usually, something would break in the house that she would have to fix or find someone to fix.

When Dad was admitted to the hospital in Halifax, Mom took us on the weekends to visit Dad. It would have been easier for her to leave us with someone, but she didn't. We always went with Mom. It would be hard to meet a stronger and braver woman than her. Many women would not bring young children to spend most of a weekend sitting in a hospital room. We were a family who stuck together through thick and thin.

∞

I hope I've captured your attention this long and you're still reading. You may be inclined to believe I had a sad childhood. The truth is I had a great childhood. My brother mostly let me tag along where ever he went. My parents loved us a lot and tried to make every situation still enjoyable for us. Going to the hospital was no different.

A Little Faith

"If God brings you to it, He will bring you through it."

Anonymous

On Mom's mediocre salary, sometimes even only an unemployment cheque, and Dad's measly annual income of less than $7000 from his disability support, there wasn't a lot of money to cover the cost of traveling. Mom and Dad really had to budget when they could. The funny thing is, we always made it to where we needed to go. Mom calls it faith.

Having faith doesn't give you permission to do stupid things. You don't ignore your problems. If you can afford to fix your car, you don't wait until next week because the timing is better. Having faith means you trust that God will take care of you when you need Him the most. If the engine light came on when Mom couldn't afford to get it fixed, the solution was simple, ignore it and hope it's nothing serious. The car is leaking oil? Not a big deal, buy a case of cheap oil. The heater stopped working? Better bring a blanket so we can keep warm. The car is making a funny noise? It's a good thing the car has a radio.

"Are we going to get there okay?" Landon would often ask Mom.

"Why wouldn't we?" Mom would reply as if Landon had asked the silliest of questions.

There were many times we relied on our faith and a little luck to get us through. One trip we had to make to Halifax was near Christmas time. There was snow on the ground, and the clouds were grey, surely, I figured it promised to be a nasty trip. Mom was nervous about driving over to Nova Scotia, especially the drive on the Cobequid Pass, a section of a highway that always seemed to storm, even in the summer.

We didn't have the money to go. It was one of many trips we were making around that time, and payday was only in a week's time for Mom. Mom had no other choice but to ask her mother to lend her some money. She didn't want to. She already had asked her mother for money a few weeks before. Mémé was not a rich lady and Mom believed there was a humiliation associated with a grown married lady still relying on her mother for financial support. No one wants to be that relative always needing money but Dad had been laying in the hospital for weeks, with no visitors except us on the weekends. It was important to keep Dad's spirits high. We had to find the money to go.

Mom, Landon, and I were almost out the door when the phone rang. It was our neighbor who wanted us to drop in for a minute before we left.

"We can't be long," Mom warned us. "We still have to go to Mémé's before we head to Halifax."

When we got to our neighbors' house, they had two brown grocery bags full of groceries for us. There were enough groceries we wouldn't have to eat out all weekend long. The bags contained just about everything we needed and wanted inside.

"We know things have been difficult for you," one of our neighbors said. "We can't fix your problems but we hope this helps."

When we were inside the car, we checked out the bags. For Landon and me, it was like Christmas had come early. There were treats that Mom only bought around the holidays. Mom had found herself a little miracle. Inside one of the bags, in an envelope, we found a hundred dollars. Mom didn't have to ask Mémé for money.

∞

Dad often had consultations in Halifax. Often, Dad would go alone or bring me with him. Mom still had to work and couldn't go with him.

"We will have to cancel, Trevor. We just can't afford it right now, and I'm not asking anyone for the money. They might be able to give you another appointment in a few weeks," Mom said.

"Don't worry," Dad responded. "We will find the money one way or another."

Mom didn't bother arguing with him. It didn't matter. She didn't have the money nor would she get the money by the time of his appointment. If he didn't want to reschedule, it would be Dad's problem to figure out.

No one mentioned the trip for several days. Finally, the appointment was the following day and Mom had no choice but to acknowledge it.

"Did you get the money?" Mom asked.

"Not yet!" Dad replied. "But I will, or I will have to ask my parents."

That afternoon someone pulled in the driveway. He saw an old junked car inside the garage when the door was opened the day before and wondered if Dad would be interested in selling the car for $200. It was enough money for Dad to go to Halifax.

∞

Another time that our faith helped us was when Dad was transferred from O'Leary to Halifax. Dad refused to go by ambulance so Mom was driving him and Landon and I were going along for the drive. It was unexpected, and we were not prepared.

"What are we going to do?" Dad asked Mom, knowing we didn't have the money to go.

"We will have to try to borrow the money from someone," Mom replied, "I'll have to call my mother."

Mom packed the few things Dad had at the hospital. She listened to the instructions the nurses gave, and we were just about ready to leave. She didn't mention we had to go to Tignish to see Mémé before we could go any further.

As we were about to leave, one nurse stopped us. "We did a collection here, and we have a little something to help you with your travels."

"Thank you," Mom replied, suddenly feeling relieved.

When we got inside the car, Mom opened the envelope. We had more than enough money to go to Halifax.

∞

I remember some of the visits we made to Halifax. I don't remember all of them, but I never recall complaining about being cooped up in a small hospital room or being bored. Usually, I was so excited to see Dad and had so much to tell him that the visits never seemed long enough.

Sometimes we didn't leave the hospital room until visiting hours were over, especially if Dad was really sick. Other times we would venture to the cafeteria if we hadn't packed lunches and Dad was feeling well enough to escape his room for a bit. Usually, no trip was ever complete without a trip to the hospital's gift shop. Landon would always get a ball, and I would get crayons and a coloring book.

∞

Mom always felt guilty that Landon and I were cooped up in the hospital for most of the weekend and sometimes for several weekends in a row. One time she wanted me to stay at my uncle's house. Nena was going to the hospital with Landon and Mom, and Papa would stay behind with me. Everyone thought this was a great idea, except for me. I wanted to see Dad. I couldn't believe they were making me stay behind.

I screamed. I cried. I refused to talk to anyone after they left. I wouldn't play with my toys or eat my lunch. I planned to make everyone as miserable as I felt. I threw the biggest tantrum. It put the ones on the internet to shame. Mom would know better than to leave me behind again.

My grandfather was getting a little tired of my attitude.

"Please stop crying," Papa begged.

"I want Daddy," I screamed.

"Then go," he said exasperated, leaving me behind in the driveway as he went inside the farmhouse.

My mind was made up. If Mom refused to take me, I would walk to the hospital. I might have only been four-years-old and had no idea where the hospital was, but I was determined to find it. Needless to say, I didn't make it very far before my grandfather stopped me. By the time my mother came back, I was in tears in my grandfather's arms, kicking and screaming.

"You're going to have trouble with that one," Papa warned.

∞

Sundays were always the hardest day to visit. We knew we would have to go home and Dad would have to stay behind. As tough as it was for us, it must have been even harder for Dad. He knew he'd be alone for the next week until the weekend arrived or until he was discharged.

There were always a lot of tears when we had to go home. I would always cry. I couldn't understand why he couldn't come home. He didn't look that sick. The concept that Dad was sick was over my head. Being sick was having a cold, and he wasn't sniffling.

I blamed Mom because Dad wasn't coming home. As I may have mentioned, we only had three channels, and I secretly watched soap operas, sometimes in the afternoon. I didn't always understand everything happening, but one couple was going through a divorce. The woman would not let her husband go home, and I wondered if Mom and Dad were going through that.

I was determined to make my point clear to my mother of who I was siding with. "If you're going to divorce him," I told her through my sobs, "then I'm staying with him."

"We're not getting a divorce," Dad promised me, "but you have to go home with Mom and Landon. I have to stay here for just a little longer."

Before we left to go home, Mom cried because I was so upset and she hated leaving Dad behind. Dad began to cry because we were all crying. He was lonesome to come home, and he craved a little freedom.

Dad would reassure me he was coming home soon but it wasn't enough for me to stop crying. My whole body shook with disappointed sobs as the three of us left Dad behind.

I didn't stop crying when Landon tripped in the parking lot and skinned his knee. It oozed with blood. My tears didn't stop falling when we went to the ER to see if someone could stitch his knee. Because there was an 8-hour wait in the ER, Landon would not see the doctor there. We would be in PEI in less than 8 hours. I was still crying when Landon started to cry. He was crying because his favorite jeans were ruined beyond salvage.

Since I refused to stop crying, Mom and Landon did their best to convince me to stop. I finally settled when Mom promised me an orange pop if I stopped crying. Yes, she was the kind of mother who occasionally used bribes. I think she might have given me the world to get me to shut up and stop crying.

∞

It was always exciting when Dad came home. Sometimes if he was in a hospital far away, he would be sent closer for a while which would be okay, but it wasn't the same as when he came home. Dad was always persuasive; so, he never spent much longer in the hospital then he had to.

I never realized Dad was probably in a lot of pain. He never complained a lot about pain. If he ate supper, he usually went to the bathroom and got sick. It was never discussed. No one made a big deal about it. It was a part of what we considered a normal family supper.

I didn't always allow Dad the time to recuperate when he got home. I never left him alone. If there was any way he could get out of bed, even for a while, then he had to. My kid logic was, 'You go to the hospital because you're sick. You get better, and you come home. When you come home, you're back to normal.'

∞

My main goal in those days was to please Mom and Dad. I thought my parents were the most brilliant people who ever existed and I wanted to impress them. I was well-behaved, determined, and passionate. I rarely needed to be told twice to do something and wanted to help if I could. Sometimes helping got me in trouble.

Having a small income meant things around the house had to be patched instead of replaced. One thing Mom and Dad never seemed to replace was the lawnmower. When they did replace it, it was an older model that likely wouldn't last much longer than two summers. Every year without fail Dad would be hunting for second-hand parts. He would say, "Maybe next year we can afford a new lawnmower."

The first cut with the lawnmower was the most exciting. The cut would be long overdue. Dad had spent so much time trying to fix the lawnmower that we just hoped that it would get through the first cut. Sometimes Dad would attach the old wagon to the lawnmower, so I could have a wagon ride.

One year during one of the first cuts, a part fell from the lawnmower. Dad was ahead of the part, and I knew he couldn't see the part or maybe not even have known it fell off. I jumped off of the wagon, determined to give him the fallen part. How proud I thought he would be of me because I was helping him, but when I picked up the part he yelled at me. I couldn't make out what he was saying, so I started to cry because he was yelling at me. Then I cried even louder because the part in my hand was scorching hot. I dropped the part and ran inside and found solace with Mom because my hand was burning and because Dad yelled which, he never did. I didn't understand why he yelled. Now, of course, I do realize he wasn't mad. He just wanted me to drop what I had in my hand.

By the time we arrived at the ER at Western Hospital, I was in excruciating pain. Dad assured me he was not mad at me, but I was still shaken up and in a lot of pain. I cried and cried because of the pain. Mom asked me to please stop crying because she was afraid it was getting on everyone's nerves. Water helped with the pain. It was the only thing that helped. I must have been allergic to the topical ointment because it made the burn even worse. I imagined how I would live the rest of my life with my hand in a basin of water because I didn't want to ever take my hand out of the water. With a little bribe from Mom, with the promise of yet another orange pop and a toy at some point, I bravely took my hand out of the water and allowed the nurse to put a dressing on my second-degree burn.

It seemed like weeks I had to wear a dressing on my hand. Every night we had to go to my cousin's house, who was a nurse, so she could change the dressing. Mom worried it would scar, and I was frustrated because I couldn't play in the sandbox. Eventually, the dressing came off, and I was lucky enough to not have a scar. A lesson was learned to never pick parts up that came off moving things – especially unsafe, hot moving things like a lawnmower.

Happy

"The best and most beautiful things in the world cannot be seen or even touched – they must be felt within the heart."

Helen Keller

If you were to ask Mom who she and Dad were stricter with; Landon or me? She'd say we were treated the same. If you ask Landon or me, we would both probably say Landon.

∞

Landon always had a bedtime until he was about fourteen-years-old. He wasn't allowed to watch movies that were rated either 18 + or unrated when he was a teenager. Dad even took away a movie from him when he was a teenager. He had a 3:00 am curfew on prom night. Mom and Dad both fell asleep, and Mom isn't sure to this day if he came home on time or not.

The first Christmas that Landon came home from university, there was a huge debate, an argument one might even say; to decipher if they would let Landon enjoy an alcoholic beverage in their house with the rest of the adults during the holidays, even though he was 18 and they knew he was probably drinking some alcohol when he was away at university.

Mom and Dad had a pretty relaxed attitude when it came to me. In my early childhood, they quickly learned that I didn't require as much sleep, so they never enforced an early bedtime. The worst-case scenario, I slept in. Not a big deal when I didn't usually have a place to go the next day. I could stay up until I decided it was time to go to bed.

Landon was a pretty good brother to me. He was better than I probably deserved. I think he felt a sense of responsibility for me because Mom and Dad always had a lot to deal with. I didn't always appreciate his bossy attitude, and I wasn't usually afraid to let him know.

Landon, for the better half of our childhood, was the brain of our operations. He made the plans, and I followed directions. We were a good team, most of the time.

∞

"Wake up," Landon commanded early one Easter morning before Mom and Dad woke.

"What do you want?" I asked annoyed.

"Let's go see what the Easter Bunny brought," he suggested.

"Okay," I agreed, getting out of bed quietly.

We quietly tiptoed our way to the living room. We glanced into our baskets, careful not to touch anything.

"Let's go back to bed," Landon ordered. "Remember you can't tell Mom and Dad that we know what we are getting for Easter."

"Okay," I replied.

There were two mornings a year we ate abnormally large meals at breakfast. It was always Christmas and Easter. It was a tradition from Dad's childhood that he incorporated into ours. It was the only time no one could leave the table until everyone was finished. It was also the only time Dad insisted he wanted seconds of everything.

"Hurry up Dad," Landon moaned, "I want to see what we got for Easter."

"When I'm done eating, we'll go see," Dad said.

As both Landon and I sat and watched Dad eat every bite, we grew more impatient by the minute. It was difficult to remain seated.

"Come on Dad," I begged, "I want to play with my new doll."

The minute it was out of my mouth, I knew I was caught. Mom and Dad knew I peeked.

"How did you know you were getting a doll?" Mom questioned.

"Well," I said, trying to buy myself time to think of a good lie, "I just guessed."

"You guessed?" Dad asked.

It was all it took before I broke and confessed.

"No, Landon and I came down early and looked."

Landon and I both learned an important lesson that morning. I learned if I had kept my mouth shut, I could have played with my new doll a half-hour earlier instead of having to listen to a lecture. Landon learned not to include me in his plans.

∞

Our family was always resourceful. We had no other choice. There were four of us living on a modest one-income salary and a disability cheque. We bought the cheaper store-brand groceries, shopped for sales, and eating out at a restaurant was a big luxury.

There was no extra money for entertainment. We had to make our own. Landon and I were probably easier to please than a lot of other kids; maybe, because of the way we were brought up. In fact, I remember one of my favorite New Year's Eve memories was a year when Dad rented a VCR player and a few movies. Mom and Dad prepared their room with air mattresses, and Landon and I slept in their room. We had so much fun that Mom and Dad bought a VCR player with some of their tax rebate that year and it became a monthly tradition.

∞

Some years we didn't go anywhere for March break. The money just wasn't there, but Mom and Dad always tried to make the time special. Mom sometimes also had to work during the break, but I don't think I realized until years later that it was because of a lack of money that we couldn't always go places.

One year, Landon and I asked if we could go to a hotel for a night. It seemed like everyone we knew was going to be staying at a hotel for March break and we wanted to stay at one too. They couldn't bring us that year. Mom was working, and it just wasn't feasible that year.

"Don't worry," Dad said, "you'll have a great March break. I promise."

The next day, Dad took us down to the basement room. It used to be my uncle's bedroom when he lived with my parents, but it was just a storage area then.

Dad had a surprise for us. He had made a tent out of blankets, but this was not just any kind of tent. This was the biggest tent made from blankets I had ever seen! The blankets connected to the pipes on the ceiling to form a tepee style tent that took up the majority of the room. It was not only the biggest tent I had ever seen, but it was also the most glorious thing that I had ever seen!

We had an old cooking stove, the kind that needed a fire to heat the food. Dad had hot dogs and marshmallows, the perfect camping foods to be eaten on the card table that he had set up.

Dad had prepared games for us to play when Mom joined us after work that evening. We played the classics, Monopoly, and Sorry. It didn't take us long to discover Dad was up to his tricks of cheating. He was a chronic game cheater.

That night, before we fell asleep, Dad kicked Mom out and told us scary stories. It felt like it was an extra-special night because Mom didn't like me hearing scary stories and that night I was allowed. She always thought that I would get nightmares.

We didn't even leave the house to have a good time. All it took was parents who had a little bit of an imagination and made an effort.

∞

In the summer, we would usually go camping for two or three weekends. We usually only had a tent and the very basic camping equipment, but Landon and I didn't care. We still had fun.

We always got a site with electricity. Dad needed to plug in his pump and Mom would bring grills to cook some of our food on. Sometimes we were the only tent in a stream of fancy campers.

One night, in late August, we discovered that we were going to need a new tent. One of the poles would no longer attach to the other. Dad had patched it the best he could with black tape, but it would only hold for so long. The wind storm was not helping.

By the time morning had arrived, we were surrounded by cars that were protecting our tent. My uncle's truck was parked on one side of the tent. Our car was parked in front of the tent. Another side of the tent was protected by a camper, and someone had pulled in behind our tent.

∞

The next summer, my parents bought a camper. It was old and tiny, but it didn't have any leaks, and if we were smart, we could all fit inside with some maneuvering.

There were really no rules for the camper. In our camper, the dirt was swept outside every morning. Some of our friends who were camping had many rules for their friends. Don't wear your shoes inside. Take a shower in the campground's bathroom if you go to the beach. It didn't really seem like they were even camping.

∞

Landon and I always thought we had a pretty good life and didn't have much to complain about. We had parents who loved us. We always did something on our breaks from school, and we didn't lack for anything that we really needed.

As much fun as Mom and Dad tried to create for our family, we also had to help out when we could. We weren't the only ones who had to work. Sometimes, some of our other family members would come too, and the work wouldn't seem like work but more of an activity. We would have competitions to see who could get the most done.

When the weather got nicer, we would go to the beach and pick moss. If there was ever any job that I hated, it was picking moss. It took forever to find enough so that we could go home. I struggled to tell the difference if it was moss or seaweed. Going to the beach and not being able to swim just didn't seem fair either.

We picked blueberries in the summer which wasn't so bad after some modifications. I brought my little chair because I hated spending so much time on my knees. I also bought a Discman because I didn't want to get bored.

The money we earned was our money to get ready to go back to school. The more we picked, the more clothes we got.

Like most kids, Landon and I wouldn't have minded if we were rich. On the rare occasions that Mom and Dad bought lottery tickets, we would imagine how our lives would change if they won and we had an abundance of money. Imagining was fun.

∞

One Good Friday, Landon and I went to the early mass in French. Mom was going to the mass later in the afternoon in English. Dad wasn't feeling great; so, he was lying in bed, sleeping, and we were not to bother him unless he was really needed.

While she was gone to mass, the phone started to ring. Landon answered it. It was a man on the phone. He sounded old and near death. His voice was raspy, and he coughed several times before he even started to speak.

"I'm your mother's great half-uncle from the states," he explained.

Mom had a big family. She had many cousins that we struggled to remember how they were related to us. A great half-uncle wouldn't have been unimaginable to us.

"I was wondering if I could talk to your mother." the man said, as he struggled to find his next breath. "Is she home? I really need to talk to her right away."

Landon sensed the urgency in the man's voice, "I'm afraid not. She's at church right now."

The man on the other end of the phone coughed again.

"You'll have to call her there. It's important."

"But they don't have a phone at the church. I can't call her," Landon explained. "She should be home in about a half hour though."

The man once again coughed and started to take some deep breaths, "I'm dying," he said, "I'm not sure that I'll live that long."

Landon's eyes got as big as barrels, "You're dying—right now?"

"Yes," the man replied, after another cough, "I have a lot of money, and I wanted to give it to your mother. Do you think she'll want it?"

"Yes!" Landon replied.

"What about my house? Do you think she'll want that?" the man questioned. "It's pretty big. The house has a pool and a hot tub."

"I think she'll probably want that too," Landon answered.

"My lawyer really needs to talk to her before I die," the man said. "We need to make sure everything goes through."

"She'll be home soon," Landon promised.

"I'll give you my phone number," the man said, as he coughed again. "Get her to call the minute that she gets home."

For the next half hour, Landon told me all about the call. We talked about Mom's great half-uncle who was now our favorite family member.

"We're going to live in a house that has a pool?" I asked.

"Yeah," Landon nodded. "It's going to be great."

When Mom got home, Landon told her everything that happened. He told her about her great half-uncle who was loaded.

"How come you never told us about him?" Landon asked.

"Because I don't have a great half-uncle," Mom responded.

"You must," Landon replied. "You should call Roy. He might know what's going on."

"Landon," Mom said, "I think it was Roy who was playing a trick on you. I promise that I don't have a great half-uncle in the states."

The excitement died down. The reality came hitting us like a ton of bricks. We were victims of a prank by Mom's older brother, Roy.

Uncle Roy lived less than a ten-minute drive away from our house. After my maternal grandparents passed away, Roy took it upon himself to become the true patriarch of the extended family. With Dad in the hospital so much, Roy was good to help Mom with anything that she needed. He would arrive at the house with packages of meat that would last throughout the winter. He often called her with weather reports before we made a trip to Halifax. He would also make sure that the car was safe enough to take. A Christmas would never pass by without a family gathering at his house.

As good as Roy was to us, he was also mischievous. He liked to pull a good joke. Despite the many times he pulled his pranks, everyone couldn't help but fall for them. Landon and I were no different.

That Easter as we all gathered at Leah's house, Roy asked Landon, "Did you get that call from our rich, great half-uncle?"

Landon nodded. He had grown to accept that it was Roy by then and not some half-uncle. Still, he was hoping that there was some truth to it.

"He had some contagious disease. They burned the house and all his money. We're not getting anything from him."

Little Suzy

"No matter what happens, some memories can never be replaced."

Unknown

One of the first cars I can remember my parents owning was a little white Chevrolet Cavalier. Mom named the car Little Suzy and the name stuck to the little white car.

We had Little Suzy for years and, oddly enough, when we bought the car it had already seemed like an old car. I can even remember when we bought it.

"You ask them!" Mom said, on our way to O'Leary early one Saturday morning. "They're your parents."

"Yeah, but they'll give a better deal than what they would give me," Dad responded. "They like you better."

Mom and I were dropped off at Nena and Papa's house while Dad and Landon ran a few errands. It was Dad's way of staying out of the way while Mom asked Papa.

"Papa?" Mom asked nervously, "you have a car you don't need and we need a car. How much will you sell it for?"

Papa hummed for a second making Mom cringe, "The Paperboy is coming soon and I don't have any change for him unless I go to the store. If you pay for the paper today, the car will be yours."

Little Suzy was the best car you could ask for. It was cheap on gas and hardly ever broke down. When it broke down, there were hundreds of cars like Little Suzy in the junkyard; so, second-hand parts were no trouble to find.

My brother and I spent many hours sitting in the backseat, playing with our toys, and having the occasional spat.

"Don't look out my window!" I would say nastily to him, "and don't put your feet on my side of the car!"

I almost felt that Little Suzy had a personality of her own; like she was kind. To me, it felt as though she cared about our safety; like when the bell would ring to remind the driver they needed to put their seatbelt on.

"Don't forget to put gas in the car as soon as you get to the gas station," Dad warned Mom. She was taking me to a babysitter for the day and she was headed to work.

As we drove by the gas station and Mom hadn't pulled in, I reminded her, "Don't forget, we need some gas."

"Don't worry," Mom said. "I'm pretty sure we have enough to get to work. I'll get some gas after work."

We drove further down the road and Mom pulled into a lane.

"I think we better turn around and go back to the gas station."

As we drove toward the gas station, the car made a strange noise.

"Are we running out of gas?" I asked, nervously.

"We might run out of gas," she replied, "but we will be okay. Even if we have to walk, it's not that far."

I wasn't fond of the idea of walking. It was winter and it was cold. I didn't have mitts or a hat.

"Why don't we sing Little Suzy a song?" Mom suggested. "If we're good enough maybe we will get to the gas station without having to walk."

So, we sang all the songs I knew; Patty Cake and the Itsy Bitsy Spider, hoping that the car would make it to the gas station. Thankfully, we did.

"Little Suzy really must have liked your singing."

Little Suzy stayed on the roads for several years after that. One day, Little Suzy made her last trip. It wasn't worth the money or time to fix her.

Elementary School

"In school, you're taught a lesson and then given a test. In life, you're given a test that teaches a lesson."

Tom Bodett

When I went to kindergarten, it was still not part of the public-school system. Mom and Dad paid for me to go. As poor as we were, Mom and Dad both felt it was very important to start on the right foot; and I needed all the help I could get.

There was a class every morning during the week, and there was an afternoon class. Mom and Dad let me pick which class I wanted to go to, and I chose the morning class.

In kindergarten and grade one, I was lucky enough to have my partner-in-crime, my cousin. We were born only three days apart and close enough that a few people mistook us for twins. Such an assumption was crazy to both of us. He was taller, I was older, and we didn't have the same parents.

"I'm getting my presents first," I'd taunt him just before our birthdays. "I'm also going to get my license before you when I turn sixteen."

"You know what they say," Landon said, trying to comfort my cousin one day, "born three days earlier, die three years earlier."

I'm not sure why but I believed almost everything I was told back then. Since we were still so young and death was still scary, I began to cry. I didn't want to die three years before him. I only wanted to get my driver's license before him.

"He doesn't know who will die first," Mom said, trying to stop me from crying.

"Don't listen to your brother. Just play and enjoy yourself," Mom warned, probably just wanting to enjoy her cup of tea with her sister and forget that she had children.

My cousin was like a security blanket. I always had someone to play with at recess time, and I never had to find a partner. Every day in grade one for our reading time, we would choose our little books, go to the same spot we always did and read to each other. It was perfect until the second month into grade one, and the teacher separated our desks, where we had once sat together, and told us we had to find new partners. Even when our names were drawn from the can, and we were supposed to be partners, she would put one name back. I was devastated and demanded Mom go into that school and make things right. Mom saw the teacher's point and thought we should make more friends. I wasn't on board with the plan.

Elementary school had its high and low points, starting on a low point my very first day. On my very first day of first grade, I left my lunch behind on the school bus. Thankfully, I had an awesome big brother who shared his lunch with me. First grade was the only grade I was ever in the same school with Landon, and I was pretty lucky to have him. Every morning he would walk me to my class.

When recess started on my very first day of school, I could not find my locker. All the lockers in the hallway looked identical, closed with only a small shower hook. Every locker in that row had to be opened to find my coat. That first day, my awesome big brother spent the entire fifteen-minute break inside the school, trying to help me find my locker.

It took a while for my brain to develop and I was behind the rest of my classmates. I seemed to be behind my classmates in almost everything. In the first grade, four of us were removed from the class for a little extra help. As the years progressed through elementary school, I was the only one who went for extra help. The others no longer needed the help or stayed behind a grade. I was in the middle where I made it to the next grade but still needed the help.

My fine motor skills needed to be refined. No matter how hard I tried, my fingers would not wrap around the pencil in the correct way, and the school had a fit. Even though I still could write, it wasn't the right way, and my fingers had to adjust. For years, I was given little devices to wrap around my pencil to make me hold it in the correct manner. Teachers made it their mission to get me to hold a pencil right. It's funny because I've noticed lately that my fingers reverted back to the old incorrect way of holding a pencil.

I wasn't good at sports. I struggled to see the ball coming towards me. I had poor vision caused by a lazy eye. For many years, I did manage to fool many people including myself and a doctor, that my eyes had perfect sight. I probably knew how bad my eyes were and didn't want to admit it then, but it was years before I got glasses. When the ball finally got close enough for me to see it, instead of trying to hit or catch it, I would blink. I was terrified that the ball would hurt, even if it was soft.

Mom was determined to find a sport I was good at and she put me in figure skating. It was a non-contact sport. My cousins were in it, and I could get free skates from them. I didn't have flat feet like my brother or father, and I didn't mind wearing skates. The only issue was Mom and Dad constantly had to tie my skates because I always took them off. My feet seemed to get itchy the moment the skates were tied.

Mom wanted me to be athletic in something, but skating was also not for me. I skated dragging one foot behind me and only lifting the other foot. Three years of expensive skating, including summer and spring break day camp, and Mom was finally willing to admit that I was indeed not going to become the next Tonya Harding.

I was a fast reader, which came in handy. My comprehension was decent. It was late to develop, but as a French Immersion student, you only read English books of any kind in the fourth grade.

Sometimes I didn't understand my style of writing. At a summer camp for 4-H, there was a competition to write an excerpt about camp. The grand prize was a notepad and a pen. I just had to win! I spent that afternoon in the mess hall, writing. That evening when they announced the winner, they announced that it was a poem. *Darn*, I thought, *wish I would have written a poem*. Imagine my surprise when I was the winner, and that notepad and pen were mine. They thought my writing was a poem.

∞

Mom was constantly changing jobs when I was young. Because of budget cuts at the hospital, she lost her position as she was not that high on the totem pole. Someone that was hired the same day could keep the job, only hours before Mom. I bet Mom wished that she would have asked for the first appointment for an interview.

She worked with several doctors, each one deciding to leave the area. Usually, they gave her plenty of notice before they left, but one did not give her that much notice.

"He's firing me," she said glumly. "He's moving his practice."

DID I TAKE THE WRONG ROAD?

"No," I panicked.

I thought being fired was a whole lot worse than what it was. I thought they would put her in a room full of fire, kind of like I pictured hell to be.

When I explained why I did not want her to get fired, she smiled and realized that it could be worse. When she explained what it meant to be fired, I thought she was overreacting. Who wouldn't want to be fired? She could stay home all the time.

It was a good time to be off from work because Dad was in and out of the hospital a lot around that time. It gave her a chance to visit and not have us kids in the way because we still had to go to school.

The Scare

"Family isn't an important thing. It's everything."

Michael J. Fox

Landon was always good at getting what he wanted from Mom. He could convince her to do exactly what he hoped she would do and convince her it was her idea.

"Mom?" Landon said. We were on our way to school one morning after we begged and pleaded to go with her to see Dad but Mom was still insisting we could not go with her. "There is a bake sale at school today and you didn't make us anything to take. It will be more expensive for you to take us to school than to take us with you. It'll also be hard to find something to bring for the bake sale now."

"I guess you can come with me," Mom eventually said, still not pleased that we weren't going to school.

It was during one of those days which Landon had convinced Mom we didn't need to go to school that Mom probably wished she would have sent us. My memories of that day are sporadic. Some of it is clear, and there are other parts I had to be reminded about.

I was in the first grade, and it seemed Dad had been sick a lot during that period. He had been in and out of the hospital a lot. In fact, he had just gotten home from the hospital in Halifax. That day felt different from all the other times we visited. It was a little more serious. The nurses wouldn't even let us see Dad when we wanted to.

Landon, Mom, and I were in a waiting room. There were a television and a payphone in the room. The room was empty, besides us.

Mom was making a lot of calls to Nena, her sister, and Mémé on the payphone. She spoke in a hushed tone and seemed distracted and upset. Landon and I were left to watch TV and play with the toys we brought.

A doctor came into the room.

"Mrs. Yuill?"

Mom stood.

"Yes."

"It's not good," the doctor said. "He'll probably not make the night."

Landon stood quickly.

"What do you mean he won't make the night?" He glanced at Mom. "He isn't God. He doesn't get to make those kinds of decisions."

"Shh," Mom tried to comfort us. "We will talk about this later, Landon. Let me talk to the doctor."

"I'm sorry," the doctor said as he looked at Landon and then me. "I didn't realize they were your children."

"I want to see Dad," Landon demanded.

"I don't think it's a good idea," the doctor replied.

Another doctor standing nearby interrupted, "I can take you two to see your Dad."

Dad was in a different room than any of the other times. It was large. I know now he was in the ICU. There were other patients in the room but Dad was in the bed against the far wall. He was connected to many different machines. The machines hummed and beeped every so often, reminding us how grave the situation was. A nurse stood close monitoring the machines and Dad. Dad was still conscious and, to us, he was still Dad. He wasn't a man who was going to die.

"Do you know what that crazy doctor said, Dad?" Landon asked as he sat on Dad's bed. "He thinks you're going to die. Isn't he an idiot?"

"Really?" Dad asked, wide-eyed. He wasn't aware of how serious his condition was.

"Do you think I can talk to your mother alone?" Dad asked. "Can you take your sister to the waiting room for a few minutes?"

Landon nodded and I reluctantly got off the bed to follow him.

"Do you think Dad will be okay?" I asked Landon.

Landon nodded, "Dad will be okay."

Dad had an infection caused by his TPN site. TPNs were a way for Dad to get nutrition without his stomach being involved. The TPNs went through a vein. He usually tolerated TPNs well, but they required strict sterile procedures. When Dad was rummaging around in the garage and using his tools, full of oil and likely dirt, he wasn't completely following the strict sterile protocol.

The infection was causing his carotid arteries to block, and blood was not moving freely from his head to the rest of his body and his head had swelled severely. He was at a high-risk of having a stroke. We needed to have luck on our side because resources on PEI were limited and technology was not as advanced as it is now.

I don't remember much more from that afternoon, but I remember Mom sending us home. Friends of Nena and Papa drove Nena down and they were driving us to Papa's house.

"Please Mom," Landon said. "Let us stay here. Don't make us go. We want to stay here with Dad."

"You can't," Mom told us, sadly. "I promise I will call if there is any news. Please Landon, just go with them and take care of your sister. Don't make me worry about the two of you."

When we got to Papa's house, my paternal grandfather's house, it was late. I was tired, scared, but glad I had my big brother beside me. Most of the time, especially when we were home, I didn't appreciate Landon bossing me around. Away from home, however,

I was grateful to have him. I knew I was safe and he would make sure everything was okay. Landon always made sure I was taken care of.

∞

Papa was having a hard night. Children aren't supposed to die before their parents. It's not right, no matter how old the child is. Dad, despite how sick he was, was no exception to the rule.

He was also dealing with his own emotional and physical pain. He was dying himself. I didn't know it at the time, but he had cancer. Papa was only in his early sixties when the colon cancer was diagnosed, and it had spread quickly. They hadn't given him a lot of time. The doctors believed he would die within six months from the time of diagnosis. It was a kick in the teeth for a man who hadn't even retired yet.

No one in the family immediately told Dad that Papa was sick and had cancer. Dad was in the hospital in Halifax when Papa was diagnosed. Dad was battling a different infection at the time. His blood needed to be cleaned by a centrifuge; which meant that they were taking the blood out from his body by a machine and cleaning it and then it was going back into his body.

Nena didn't want Dad to have anything more to deal with. Mom didn't like being dishonest with Dad but respected Nena's wish and agreed to keep it quiet for the time being. Mom would not lie if he asked point blank about what was going on, but she would not offer any information.

Dad knew something was going on at home. He was good at reading between the lines. He hadn't heard from his father for a while and his mother sounded distant when they were talking. Mom tried to change the topic when they were talking about his parents.

"What is going on?" Dad asked Mom on the phone. "Why is my father still in the hospital?"

"You'll have to talk to your mother. I'm not really sure about everything that's going on," Mom told him. She tried to change the topic before they broached any further with the subject.

Dad sighed, understanding Mom's difficult predicament, "Don't worry about it, Lorna. Mom sounds distant. She doesn't want you to tell me, and I will not put you in the middle of this. I'll deal with it."

"I spoke to my doctor this evening and he is going to let me come home tomorrow. Will you be able to come and get me in the morning?"

"Sure," Mom said, excited to get him home.

The next morning, Mom packed us in the car, and we made our way to Halifax. We only had to drive into the parking lot, and Dad came out.

"Is everything okay?" Mom asked. Usually, she had to go to the floor, sign papers, and listen to the instructions from the nurses. This differed from any of the other times.

"Yeah," Dad said, as he got behind the wheel.

On the way home from Halifax, we stopped at the hospital in Summerside. Dad and Landon went inside while Mom and I waited in the car.

When Dad came out, he was angry. Not too many words were exchanged on the way home as he stared motionlessly ahead.

That evening, Nena called Mom.

"Trevor doesn't look great."

"No, but he must have been good enough to be discharged from the hospital," Mom replied.

"His brother was in to visit him the other day," Nena said. "Dana can't believe they let Trevor go. According to him, he was nowhere near ready to be discharged when he was there."

Mom hung the phone up. Thoughts started to ramble in her mind. Something was not making sense. She started talking to Dad about how he had improved so rapidly. It was almost a miracle how quick they let him go home. Eventually, he told her the truth. He signed himself out, against medical advice.

Not long after Dad had been admitted to Summerside because of the TPN infection and he was in the ICU.

The doctors had a busy night with Dad. They kept in contact with specialists in Halifax for most of the night. With a little luck and a lot of prayers, Dad pulled through.

Things were looking brighter the following day. Dad was probably going to be okay. He had to take blood thinners for years after, which carries a hefty risk. He may have bled out if he had fallen or had any other injuries. It also became harder to get access to get lines for IVs which really played a key factor in some of the health struggles Dad faced after that.

I don't really remember Dad's recovery from that particular incident. To me, it was like he was sick one day and almost fully recovered the next. Mom believes it was more like a week of time to recuperate in the hospital and he recuperated for a while when he got home.

"Thank the Lord, we got our miracle," Mom would say when we would reminisce about it.

"I'll probably never be so lucky again," Dad often said. "That was my chance."

The Car We Barely Had

"Sometimes you will never know the value of a moment until it becomes a memory."
                                            Dr. Seuss

We needed a car so Mom called her brother Roy to see if he knew of any cars that were for sale. He had a station wagon he wasn't using anymore. He sold it for a good price, $500, but it needed a little work.

I think it was around the end of September that we bought the car. One Saturday morning, after the four of us had a bite to eat for breakfast, we made a plan to go to Uncle Roy's house, so Dad could work on the car.

I begged Mom to let me stay home. It seemed like such a long bicycle ride, and my bicycle was second-hand and my legs weren't really long enough to reach the pedals without having to strain my legs. Since I was only about 7-years-old, Mom wouldn't let me stay home alone.

We took a dirt road to make the drive quicker, but it was still pretty slow driving. It probably took less than an hour, but it seemed to take forever. Every time we reached a small hill, I would be scared that I would fall off my bike; so, I got off and walked the bike up and down the hill.

Mom had broken her leg a few years before, and she didn't have all the strength to do the 4 kilometers or more on a bike ride. Dad didn't have the energy either.

Mom tried to pass the time by talking.

"Someday you guys will have kids of your own and you can take them for a bike ride," Mom said.

"I hope my wife has four kids," Landon said.

"I'm lucky, I can have my own kids," I retorted, a little proud of my ability.

Landon had to defend himself and said, "But your kids won't be Yuills and mine will be."

"What?" I said, shocked. "Why won't my kids be Yuills, Mom?"

"Because once you get married, you won't be a Yuill anymore," Mom explained.

"Who will I be?" I asked, not sure if I really wanted to hear the answer. It was a shocking revelation that I was just not prepared for.

"It depends on who you marry," Landon uttered. "You'll take his last name."

"That's not fair!" I exclaimed, "I don't want to change my last name. I want to keep it."

If I didn't keep my last name, I would be the only one in my family to have a different last name. I would be an outsider, and that just didn't seem fair.

"You can keep your last name if you really want," Mom promised, "but you may feel differently when you get married. I took your father's last name."

"I won't feel different," I boasted, "I'll always want to be a Yuill."

"A new last name could bring you some luck," Dad advised.

"How?" I asked.

"Well, I never heard of a famous Yuill before," he pointed out, "I don't even know of any Yuills who are really rich."

I took a moment to think about what he was saying. I had big plans, at a young age, to hit it rich, and I wanted nothing to hold me back. Maybe a last name wasn't really that important?

"Maybe you guys are right," I agreed. "I think I should change my name as soon as I turn 18."

It only took about two afternoons for the old station wagon to be ready to be brought home. It worked better than ever, and although it was old, I thought it was one of the best cars we ever owned.

One night that week, Dad and I went to pick up Mom and to pick up my skates that were just sharpened when we were hit by a bus. The school bus lost control, something to do with its brakes, and it could not stop. Our car, that Dad spent more time working on than getting to drive, was automatically written off by the insurance company. It was gone but at least Dad and I were okay.

Growing Up Catholic

"Prayer is bringing your wishes and worries to God; faith is leaving them there."

Anonymous

Growing up in a fairly strong Catholic family meant there were a few pretty strong traditions we stuck to. Every Lent, for the duration of the 40 days and 40 nights, we would try our hardest to give something up as a sacrifice. Usually, Mom would convince Landon and me to give up all junk food.

During the Holy Triduum, we would go to church on Holy Thursday, Good Friday, and Holy Saturday. Even at a young age we still had to go when these masses were long and hard to understand. Plus, Holy Saturdays didn't finish until it was really late at night.

Every time we passed by a church, we made the sign of the cross. Even if I wasn't sure it was a Catholic church or if it was even a church at all, I still made the sign of the cross. It was better to be safe than sorry.

Christmas meant recognizing that it was more than a commercial holiday. The meaning of Christmas was the birth of Jesus. Hence, abbreviating Christmas to Xmas in our family was as bad as forgetting to check the oil in a car before a long trip and forgetting to check the oil in a car could almost be compared to attempted murder in Dad's eyes.

Being brought up as a Catholic means that second grade is a very important year of religion classes. It's the year that kids usually make their first confession and join the church congregation to receive communion for the first time.

I wasn't so keen on making my confession. The idea of having to go into a room and tell the priest everything you have done wrong just wasn't something I was excited about – or even into at all. I'm still not fond of confessions, but I enjoy the healing aspect of having God's love and forgiveness after a confession.

For me, my first communion was so much more important than just getting communion. It was another thing I would be able to do that everyone else in my family could already do.

Being the youngest in a family means having to wait your turn for everything. Since Landon was five years older than I was, it seemed like I was always the odd one left out.

First Communion, as exciting as a time as it can be, can also be expensive for parents. Parents have to buy their children clothing to wear. The girls usually wear little white dresses and the boys wear suits. Hair appointments are usually needed for the little girls and usually a gift would have to be bought.

My parents were getting off lucky because a great-aunt of Dad's, whom I had only met once, made me a beautiful white dress. I felt like a little princess in the dress. It was an original, made with my measurements. It was a dress that couldn't be found in the catalogs that came in the mail.

The best part of the dress was that it was saving my parents about $50 when $50 was really needed. I hoped we could use the $50 for something fun to do or I would get another gift.

I had the dress, but I still needed the shoes. Two weeks before my First Communion, Mom ordered a pair of white dress shoes from the catalog, but three days before my First Communion, they still hadn't come in. Panic was setting in for Mom. What would she do if the shoes didn't come in?

Nena went to the second-hand store in O'Leary to see if they would have a pair of shoes that would do. The only fancy shoes they had in my size were a pair of shiny black dress shoes with a bow on the top. The black shoes were supposed to be meant only as a last resort if the white shoes didn't come in before my big day.

Well, the white shoes came in on the day of my First Communion. Dad picked them up, but I refused to wear them. The black shoes were actually comfier to wear, and I knew they cost a lot less than the white pair.

"Why won't you wear the white shoes?" Mom pleaded.

It was a lost cause. I had already decided that I would only wear the black shoes and Mom learned that she had to pick her battles.

Mom and Dad were never picture-taking kinds of people. They were more of the people who bought a camera, put the camera away, and spent more time looking for the camera than using the camera. If they used the camera, they would change the film and put the film bottle in the cupboard and then probably never get the film developed.

For my first communion, Mom and Dad borrowed Nena's Polaroid camera to take pictures. It was a new camera and Dad had never used it before and didn't look at it until we got to the church. Not really a great place to fiddle with a camera.

Dad took a picture to see if the camera would work. As the flash on the camera went off, the talking camera loudly spoke, "He shoots, he scores!"

"Dad!" Landon said, embarrassed. "Don't take any more pictures. Shut it off."

I was too young to be embarrassed. I thought it was funny that everyone was looking around to see what was making the noise, but Landon's face was getting redder and redder. Dad was still fiddling with the camera, trying to find a way to shut off the sound, when he accidentally took another picture and once again, the camera spoke.

Dad put the camera down. He would try to take more pictures after the mass ended.

Mom passed me a piece of gum because she wanted to make sure I had fresh breath.

It was the best kind of gum, *Double Bubble*. It was full of sugar. We never had a lot of gum. It just wasn't something we bought, so I wasn't great at chewing gum. Mom only carried it around in case Dad had a bout of low blood sugar.

I was a loud gum chewer and it used to bother me when I had gum, but I never seemed to be able to blow a bubble. Mom, Dad, and Landon all could. Without even thinking of where I was, I tried to blow a bubble with my gum.

"Atara!" Mom said, in one of her tones that could make hair stand straight but only loud enough for me to hear it. "Stop blowing bubbles and swallow that gum."

I knew better than to question her. I tried to swallow the gum, but it got stuck halfway down my throat. I started to cough to help it along, and because it was irritating, my eyes were watering, and I began to panic and wonder if the gum would ever be swallowed. I coughed again. This time it went down, and I breathed a sigh of relief.

If I were to look back at most of the pictures taken that day, my eyes were roaming or I was blinking. I was neither smiling nor was I even looking at the camera, but the one thing that drew me apart from all the other little girls was my black shoes in a row of white.

When I was in the fifth grade, I began altar serving at mass. When you're a kid, it's tough to sit in a pew for an hour. When you're really young, you can bring toys to mass; but there comes a time when you have to sit still. You are still a child because you're still about ten-years-old and the significance of the mass is still not fully comprehended. If you were an altar server, you had a chance to move around and still serve God.

I altar served a lot with my brother. He made sure I did the job and didn't forget anything. Most of the time it worked great. He made sure I didn't look like a fool and I didn't forget anything. There were other times I disliked his bossy attitude.

One week I was amazed by how beautiful and silky my hair was. I was never impressed by my hair. It seemed like it was always a mess of curls and tangles. But that particular day, I was having a good hair day.

It always seemed hard to get a good hair day. Most people we knew didn't have straighteners, and it was too hard and time-consuming for me to use a curling iron. All one could hope for it seemed was that their hair came out somewhat nice after a shower.

"Put your hair in a ponytail," Landon ordered when we were at the back of the church waiting for the mass to begin.

"No!" I responded when shaking my head. Today wasn't a day I planned to listen to his orders. I was a free spirit who enjoyed my long wavy hair. I liked when I moved my head, and my hair swayed. I wanted to shout to the world, 'Look at my hair. It's so pretty!'

When the mass began, we walked towards the altar. I was still amazed at how curly my hair was, and I loved how it swayed to the rhythm of my walk. I moved my head again, but I moved it a little too close to the candle I was holding. Before I knew it, my hair caught on fire.

I started to blow on my hair, but the fire wouldn't stop. It wasn't spreading, but I was panicking. A part of my body was literally on fire.

"Landon!" I said a little louder than I should have.

Without much hassle, he was able to blow the fire out of my hair, but I had to sit through mass, smelling my burnt, crisp hair. The appeal to sway my hair was gone.

Landon smirked as Mom had to cut a piece of my hair after mass.

"You probably should have listened to me."

Home

"Home is the nicest word there is."
Laura Ingalls Wilder

I never imagined I would end up living in West Prince. Living on PEI wasn't even supposed to be a part of the plan. As a child, I constantly begged and pleaded with my parents to move to a big city; however, they did not share the same enthusiasm about city living as I did. They liked living near their family and friends. They also liked how they knew mostly everyone who lived in the area. If they didn't know a person, they knew their parents, grandparents, or someone they could make a connection with.

Every time Mom and Dad would ask me to help take in the wood for the winter or help shovel the car out on a cold and blustery day, I would remember the plan I made. My plan was easy. After I graduated from high school, I would make my move to a big city, probably New York. I would find an amazing apartment with a doorman whose name would be George. I wouldn't have to shovel snow, take in wood, or even mow the lawn. Every day I would go to work at a big office and do whatever people in offices did. Mom and Dad could come to visit. I'd even let Landon come if he wanted.

What I failed to realize was how much I grew to love and appreciate West Prince. It was a unique place to live. A trip to the grocery store for milk and bread could take Mom a long time by the time she got through talking to everyone. We often wave in traffic because we usually know who it is. Once when I was walking down my road for exercise, I was asked three times if I wanted a drive home because it looked like rain. You're never stuck long on the side of the road before someone stops to help – not being the daughter of my parents, anyway. I swear they knew everyone.

It was when I went away to camp one summer that I realized how much I liked home. It wasn't my first time away. I had gone to other camps before, but the camp I attended between the 5th and 6th grade was the longest I had ever been away from home. The camp was about ten days long, and I was over the moon with excitement.

From the second I found out I was going, I made a list of what I would need to bring. I packed my bag a week before I was going and every day I unpacked to make my suitcase a little neater. I cleaned my room because I wanted to come home to an immaculately clean bedroom. I even ironed my bed and slept on the couch until it was time to go to camp.

∞

Two days before I left, I had a mishap that almost caused me not to go to camp - I lost my glasses.

"We should go to the beach," Landon suggested. "We could go for a swim and then have a bonfire."

"Okay," I agreed.

When we went to the beach, I happily jumped into the water. I only stopped when the water came to my neck. I quickly dunked under the water to stay warm.

When it was time to get out and warm up by the fire, I noticed something was off. I couldn't find my glasses. Panic set in. I needed my glasses.

I searched my beach bag and the vehicle. I couldn't find them. Reality was hitting home. The only explanation was I must have gone swimming with my glasses on.

"What am I going to do?" I asked.

Glasses were expensive, especially mine. I needed strong lenses, and Mom and Dad had to pay to get them thinned. They only got me one pair to help cut the cost. I couldn't see well without them. Sometimes I even struggled to find them in the morning when they were on my night stand. My head would pound if I didn't wear them. How was I going to go to camp?

"There isn't anything you can do about it now," Mom said that night. "You might as well relax tonight and go to sleep."

The next morning, Mom became a woman with an important mission - finding me a set of glasses. She said a little prayer to God and made the necessary phone calls. She begged and pleaded, and her hard work paid off. I would have to sacrifice my bifocal lenses, but I could get my distance lenses in time to go to camp.

∞

When the bus came to pick me up for camp at the designated parking lot, I hopped on the bus without so much as a goodbye to my parents. I waved from my seat and couldn't wait to get to camp.

On the first night after I listened to the camp rules and the strict schedules and routines, the reality of being away from home hit me. I missed being able to take my shower when I wanted or go to bed when I felt like it. I began to wonder if the whole camp experience was really for me. The more I thought about home, the more I missed home. I missed my dog. I was even beginning to miss Landon. My biggest worry was that Mom and Dad would do something fun and I wouldn't be there.

I decided it was time to take action. I wanted to go home, but I had been at enough camps to know it would not be easy. They didn't just let you go home because you wanted to. I wasn't even allowed to make a phone call to my parents and beg them to pick me up. I was going to have to be creative if I wanted to go home.

I struggled to come up with my plan and fall asleep as the other girls snored loudly in the cabin. I was suddenly very grateful my parents only had two children, and equally grateful that I didn't have a sister.

I knew I wouldn't have liked to share my room. With much thought, I came up with the perfect plan. I could finally fall asleep soundly knowing I would go home sometime the next day.

The next morning, I asked to speak to my counselor in private. I had something really important to tell her. As I had rehearsed it in my head the night before, I told her I got my period for the very first time and I needed to go home. However, she did not see it as the same emergency as I had envisioned she would. She told me I would be fine. She passed me a bag of supplies and reminded me not to go swimming for a few days.

I was devastated. My fail-proof plan failed. Not only did my plan fail but now I wouldn't be able to go swimming. Swimming was my favorite activity. I had to come up with a better plan. A plan guaranteed to get me sent home.

I thought about trying to phone home secretly, but the only phone on the whole camp was in the director's office. We weren't allowed into the director's office unless we were invited and I was not a kid who could break the rules easily. If I did, my heart would race and I would panic before I even started. Breaking into the director's office in the middle of the night when no one was around was tempting but not an option.

By that afternoon, I was absolutely homesick. I missed home more than I knew was possible. I sat outside the mess hall because the kitchen staff played the same radio station Dad always insisted we listen to.

Dad only listened to classic rock, and most of the time I found it annoying but I sure was missing it then.

∞

My thoughts changed when I met a boy that afternoon. It made me question my beliefs as I wondered if I had wrongly judged the whole camp experience. Maybe camp was for me, after all.

Since I considered myself to be a modern-day woman, I didn't hesitate to make the first move. I sent a girl from my cabin to see if he may have feelings for me. I would have denied the whole thing and made him believe it was all a joke or a misunderstanding.

The girl pointed me out to him because he had no idea who I was. He knew a good catch when he saw one, and we began our relationship.

It all started by the picnic table. We got to know one another. I took his picture and found someone to take our picture together because I couldn't wait to go home and show Mom.

For two days, the two of us were in a beautiful relationship. We chose the same activities every day. None of the camp counselors even bothered to question why I could swim, and I didn't mention it.

Alas, there was trouble in paradise. A girl from my cabin stole him right from under my nose. Apparently, they had more in common than we did because they were both going to junior high and I was still in elementary school.

I wondered how I was supposed to have reacted to the situation. If I was a woman on a soap opera, I'd have to slap the other woman. Instead, I asked myself, what would *Felicity King* on *Road to Avonlea* do? Felicity was my favorite character on the show, and a very *'Felicity King'* thing to do would have been to write a letter and express my emotions.

I rummaged through my bag trying to find the paper, pens, and envelopes I packed. I expected when I packed to go to camp, I would write a letter home every day, but I hadn't written one letter home.

I couldn't find the paper I packed, but I found the envelopes. I wrote my letter, filled with emotions that I really wasn't feeling but thought I should be, on the back of an envelope. I don't remember what I wrote, but I sure wish I still had a copy of that letter I wrote.

Their relationship hadn't ended well, and I couldn't help but smile a little when I heard about it. I was stubborn and decided I didn't care for either of them at that point; so, I did my best to stick my nose up at both of them and ignore them.

On the bus when we were leaving camp, I sat directly across from him. I wondered if I should get his phone number or at the very least, his e-mail, just for old time sakes. We were in a relationship for about two days after all.

As tempted as I was to ask, I didn't. Some things are better left at summer camp. I never gave him much thought again until I started writing. As silly and immature as it was, he was my first experience at a relationship.

Landon ended up going to camp, and I think it may have been the same summer. He was going away for two whole weeks to an Air Cadet Camp. I was excited to have Mom and Dad to myself.

Mom was on vacation from work when the camp was finished. Mom, Dad, and I would pick Landon up and do some camping. Mom and Dad assumed Landon was at the military base in New Brunswick near Mom's Aunt Olive and Uncle Alfred's house. They were so sure it was in New Brunswick that they never paid any attention to the forms.

The day before we were leaving, Mom decided to call Landon. She wanted to tell him what time we would be there. She also wanted him to remind her what time the closing ceremonies were.

She didn't have a phone number. She had to rely on using Directory Assistance. Directory Assistance gave her a phone number to try for the base in New Brunswick.

"I'm sorry, but we have no Air Cadets here," the receptionist told her.

"Where is my son?" She panicked. He had been gone for over a week and a half.

"The cadets all go to Greenwood in Nova Scotia," the receptionist reminded her. "No one gave you this information?"

"Yes," Mom replied. She didn't want to sound like a mother who had no idea where her kid was, so she scrambled to come up with a lie. "I misplaced the information and found this phone number. I just thought someone could direct my phone call."

"It's a good thing we found out now," Dad smiled when Mom explained what had happened. "The camp is in the opposite direction from your aunt and uncle's."

A Pain in the Neck

"The real man smiles in trouble, gathers strength from distress, and grows brave by reflection."

Thomas Paine

Just before Christmas, when I was in the sixth grade, Dad stumbled down the basement stairs late one night when he was going down to check the fire. Luckily, he didn't fall. He grabbed onto something to keep his balance, but he tightened his body enough to make his neck hurt the next day.

His neck really hurt after that night, and he seemed to be feeling run down.

He just wasn't feeling great.

After Christmas, our family doctor did some testing because Dad's neck was still sore and he wasn't feeling any better. He sent a referral for Dad to see a neurosurgeon in Moncton.

In late January, on a Friday afternoon, Dad went to Moncton. The neurosurgeon looked at some of the tests and the procedures that had been done in the past. He examined Dad and told him he would have to come back to the hospital on Sunday night to be admitted.

The doctor did not give much of a reason why Dad had to go back to the hospital to be admitted or what they were planning. Dad knew there was a strong possibility he might need surgery. His bones were weak in his neck and it was probably a result of poor nutrition. Dad wasn't overly excited about the surgery or having to go to the hospital.

On Sunday afternoon, we borrowed my aunt and uncle's car, and the four of us went to Moncton. Dad sat in the back seat beside me. Dad never sat in the backseat. Most times it would make him car sick.

It wasn't a great day for Dad. He hoped he could sleep. He took up most of the seat, trying to find a comfortable position.

Mom tried her hardest to convince Landon and me not to go. It was a Sunday, and we wouldn't get home until it was really late. We had school in the morning and we wouldn't get home until it was really late, but both Landon and I were determined we were going with them.

When it was time to leave Dad at the hospital, it was difficult.

"I'll be fine," Dad assured us.

On the way home, Mom started to cry. It had been at least a year or so since Dad had been admitted to a hospital off-island. We were cocky and thought those days might be behind us. Dad was improving health wise, but this was a setback and a major one at that.

"Mom, let me drive home," Landon begged. "You shouldn't drive right now."

Landon was a new driver and only had his beginners. In the backseat, I feared for my safety. My options were to insist Mom drive or take my chances with Landon. By the sound of Mom's blubbering, I was better off taking my chances with Landon.

"Mom!" Landon said. "Look at the car in front of us. Do you see what the bumper sticker says?"

The car in front of us, a small, old beater of a car had one bumper sticker that looked fresh, and it was easy to read. RELAX... BE HAPPY. Mom always taught us to believe in signs. She believed some signs were messages from God. It was God's way of reminding us He didn't forget about us. We needed to have faith in him. This was our sign from God. Things were going to be okay. Dad was going to be okay.

"Dad won't be in the hospital for long," Landon insisted.

It was no hidden secret that Dad wasn't exactly fond of hospitals. He told his fair share of lies to get out of them over the years. He wouldn't be there any longer than he had to be.

"Yeah," Mom joked, "I bet we will have to find someone to go and pick him up by Tuesday."

We got home late that evening.

"Get in your pajamas and go straight to bed," Mom ordered.

∞

The next morning, I woke early and went downstairs for breakfast. Mom and Landon were sitting at the table. They both looked upset.

"What's going on?" I asked, gazing at Mom and then Landon.

"Look around," Landon replied, a little bitter as he pointed around the room.

My eyes adjusted to the light of the room for the first time that morning. I started to notice something was drastically wrong. The curtains all had thick coatings of ash and dirt. The walls were now stained, and there were cobwebs in the corner. The dishes on the shelves all had thick layers of soot on them.

"What happened?" I questioned.

"I'm not sure," Mom commented, "but the house is in a mess."

"When did it happen?" I asked.

"It must have happened yesterday when we weren't here," Mom replied, "I don't think I even bothered to turn on the lights when we got home. We were so exhausted."

"What are we going to do?" I asked.

I looked around, trying to view all the damage. The house was filthy. There was a strange distinct smell. As I looked at myself in the mirror, I realized I was even coated with a layer of soot.

"We won't worry about it now," Mom replied. "I'll talk to your Dad tonight. We'll figure out what we should do about it. We need to get ready for school and work."

The only clothes we had that didn't smell or weren't full of soot, were the clothes in the dryer. For me, it was an old black shirt full of paint stains and a pair of pants that were second-hand and old when I got them. It was an appealing fashion statement I made that day!

When Mom spoke to Dad on the phone that evening, he convinced Mom we needed to go through insurance. We weren't even sure of the extent of the damage or what caused it. The entire house needed to be scrubbed from top to bottom. The walls needed to be painted, and the furniture and rugs would need to be steam cleaned. It was just too much work for Mom to organize by herself when she was working full time and Dad was in the hospital.

∞

On Tuesday morning, like we predicted, Dad asked if he could go home. He didn't even need to lie. He explained he was needed at home because of the mess, but the doctor persuaded Dad to stay a little longer. The doctor believed Dad wouldn't get very far before he seriously injured himself.

Mom was on her own to deal with the insurance company and the mess that was going on at home. The furnace had backfired, creating the mess. We were fortunate that the insurance company was good to deal with. They quickly hired a cleaning company to clean the mess in the house.

Every morning, before we left for school and work, the ladies who were hired to clean would come into our house.

To say it was a difficult time for my family is putting it mildly. It seemed like I never knew what I was coming home to lose. Every night we would be greeted by what seemed like dozens of garbage bags of things they couldn't save which included my extensive teddy bear collection, bears that had multiplied into the hundreds.

Landon collected farm sets. To most people, they looked like toys, but they weren't to Landon. He didn't play with these sets. He modeled the small-scale farm set. He took pride in positioning every tractor, animal, and figurines included in the set. He had racked up quite the collection over the years.

"They're just things," Mom reminded Landon and me. "We can replace them."

The ladies also disconnected the wires hooked to the television, and we lost our satellite. We only had one receiver, but there were four televisions connected to that receiver. Hidden behind the floor model television were hundreds of wires which only God and Dad knew what their purpose was for.

Dad had connected the receiver, so each room was lucky enough to have a connection. We all had to watch the same things which led to a few arguments over the years, but it worked for us.

With Dad in the hospital, he couldn't reconnect the televisions. We would go without TV until Landon was brave enough to try his method of hooking the wires in one by one and seeing what would happen. It was tedious but worth it.

When the ladies were finished cleaning, and the bags of garbage were stored in the basement, Landon and me went fishing through them. Some of the things meant too much to us for us to throw them out. Mom took a few things out too.

She had very few things that survived the house fire before I was born. She was willing to put in a little elbow grease to save some of the gifts from her wedding. Some things were given to her from her parents. They were all that was left. It didn't matter if they weren't as clean and fresh looking as they once were.

∞

Dad was scheduled to have a minor surgery a few days after his admission. It was only minor and about as safe as a surgery can be; so, we didn't go.

The surgery wasn't successful. They were attempting to put a plate in his neck but the bone shattered. From what they could gather, bones in his neck had likely broken in the original accident but no scans were ever done in that particular area, and it was missed. They didn't heal properly and now because of malnutrition; the bones were weak.

Dad was put in traction. Tongs were attached to his head. The tongs had string-like attachments connected to weights. I don't remember exactly how much weight was connected, but I think it was around 10 pounds.

"I think they're trying to kill me," Dad told Mom on the phone.

"Oh Trevor," Mom sympathized, "you won't be in traction forever."

He was in traction for about 6 to 8 weeks. While he was in traction, he couldn't raise his head much. He didn't have the freedom to use his body. Dad was confined to his bed in the hospital. While he was in traction, he could only really look in one direction, toward the ceiling. He could move his body around just enough to prevent any sores from forming, but he was stuck laying on his back. Dad could really only hear the voices and see the tops of heads of people talking to him unless they got really close to him.

He was bored when we weren't there to visit with him. He didn't really know anyone there. The nurses had too much to do to keep him company. He got the occasional visitor which he was grateful for.

He couldn't do a lot of other things. It was difficult to hold books in a comfortable position so he could read them. His arms would get tired quickly. It was even difficult for him to watch television. The adjustable television did not adjust enough for him to see it well.

∞

The first weekend we went to visit, we left on a Friday evening after Mom was done with work for the day. Visiting hours were over by the time we got there. All we could do was pop our heads in Dad's room and wish him good night.

Someone had told Mom that the hospital had a hostel in the basement. It was cheap and clean, but it certainly wasn't a four-star rating. The room was only the size of a small bathroom or a good-sized walk in closet. It was furnished with old hospital beds, and a cot could be added to the room for an extra fee.

The walk to the hostel was like walking through an alternate universe. The elevators opened to a freshly painted basement level floor but the further we walked, the more the atmosphere changed. Near the elevator, clean and bright arrows were painted on the floor to give direction, but the more we walked, the more the arrows faded. The ceilings, full of pipes, gave us a true picture of the age of the building. The smell became intolerable for a short period as we passed the smoking room for the patients and visitors. The room was often full and had a strong enough odor to cause us to cough as we walked passed.

Our room had a dead bolt on the door. Mom quickly locked it when we were safely inside, and she placed a chair in front of the door. The bathroom was just down the hall so it could be a challenge to get out in a hurry.

"How are we going to do this?" Mom said, referring to the bed situations. There were three people and only two single beds.

"I'm not sharing a bed with my sister or my mother!" Landon exclaimed.

Mom and I tried to find a comfortable position on the cot for the two of us which proved impossible. It maddened me that Landon was snoring on the other side of the room, close enough for me to touch, and I couldn't sleep because I was afraid to fall off the bed.

The next weekend Mom decided we would only go over on Saturday morning. We didn't really get to visit on Friday so it would save the cost of one night in the hostel.

"Landon?" Mom asked. "Since we are only going for one night, why don't you stay in another room?"

"I think we can manage with just one room, Mom," Landon replied. Again, Mom and I tried to manage sleeping on our single bed which was proving to be near impossible. We tried to lay on opposite ends, but neither of us appreciated feet near our faces.

The next weekend, Mom had a plan. We moved both beds to the middle of the room and put them together. The three of us could easily lay in the two beds without invading personal space. Only our feet would dangle from the edges of the bed. She had thought of the plan throughout the week but failed to remember the cot and the bed were not the same height. The beds seemed to divide our torsos from our legs, and it felt awkward. The hospital bed was also on wheels with brakes that didn't work. Whenever someone would move, the beds would separate.

The floor was concrete, and no amount of blankets could attempt to make it look comfortable or warm. There wasn't enough room to bring an air mattress, but it was Dad's idea to use a swimming floatation device.

We were lucky enough to have good weather every Saturday morning when we left. On Sundays, without fail, the weather was always awful. Between bouts of freezing rain and snow, Mom drove home slowly.

We had a red Grand Prix at the time. Dad bought it with the insurance money he got from the station wagon when it was hit by the bus. The Grand Prix was ripening with age and one continuous problem we had with that car was the heater. It never seemed to work on the weekends. Mom would take the car to the garage on the first day of the week when we would get back, and they fixed it within a day or so. By the time Saturday would roll around the heater would stop working and we had to rely on heavy coats and a blanket. The car also overheated. Every half hour we would need to stop on the side of the road to give the engine a few minutes to cool down. The irony was not lost on the fact that while the engine was steaming hot, we were freezing cold inside.

Dad celebrated his fortieth birthday in Moncton while he was still in traction. The nurses who had become a part of our extended family brought him a piece of cake and found enough meals from patients who had been discharged, for us to enjoy a meal together. It was the first meal that the four of us had eaten together in weeks.

Eventually, they put Dad in a halo and despite its name, Dad didn't feel much like an angel. He would be in it for a couple of months. The halo had vertical rods that kept Dad's head fixed in one position, looking straight ahead. It was attached by small pins inserted into his skull. The rods went past his shoulders and fastened together by a belt.

With the halo, he could go home, or at least closer to home. They transferred him to the hospital in O'Leary. He was only there for a few days before he convinced the staff to send him home on a Thursday afternoon. The hospital was having an outbreak of the flu, which would cause a lot of grief if Dad were to have caught it. Reluctantly, they agreed to send him home.

He came home in such a hurry that Mom didn't have a chance to prepare. He couldn't be left alone. He couldn't get out of bed in a hurry and Mom worried he would fall. Nena was coming home from Ontario the following week but it didn't solve what they would do on Friday.

I caught the flu on Thursday night and couldn't go to school on Friday. With a mask on my face, I went into Dad's room that Friday to spend the day with him.

Our community came together and planned a benefit for our family. It wasn't hard to see we were struggling. The winter had certainly taken its toll on all of us; financially and mentally. The benefit was a great success, and it was overwhelming to know how much our community supported us.

Kindness

"What wisdom can you find that is greater than kindness?"

Jean-Jacques Rousseau

After Dad got sick, there were many times our community stepped up to the plate for us. We were extremely grateful for our neighbors, friends and family's kindness towards our family. Without them, I'm not sure how we would have ever survived.

It wasn't always money that we were given either. Prayer cards were sent to our house often, and people told us they were keeping us in their prayers. Meals were made for us. Sometimes, our lawn was cut for us. If we were stuck at the end of the driveway in the winter time eventually someone would offer a hand. We were incredibly lucky and blessed to live in the community we did.

Mom always wanted us to be grateful for the help we were getting. She didn't want us to be too proud to accept help when we needed it, but it was also important that we weren't afraid to lend a helping hand when we could.

Dad did his best by trying to be a good example for Landon and me. For him, he hoped that kindness came naturally to us. He wanted us to help people automatically and without hesitation. Dad never drove by a vehicle on the side of the road without checking if they were okay or needed something. Dad moved grocery carts in parking lots and put them where they belonged. He hated how they could bang into someone's car. Dad never wanted attention or praise if he helped someone. He wasn't the kind of guy who would stop to check on someone if four other cars were already stopped.

One of the most important lessons Dad taught me about kindness was when I was in elementary school. Every winter our school would have races at the rink. It was a part of the school's winter carnival. I competed in the races, so I wanted Dad to come and watch them. The rink was probably the last place Dad wanted to go but he always agreed to go on any field trip when I asked. I don't think I realized how much I was asking from his introverted personality until I got older.

I was lucky that day. My goal in any race was not necessarily to finish first. My main goal was just to not come in last, and I achieved it that day. I finished smack dab in the middle. To finish around the middle was equivalent to coming in first place for me. I was thrilled with my result.

Another girl, in a different competing level, did come in last. All of the other kids in her level were off the ice, and she still wasn't finished. They say kids can be cruel and they were. They were laughing at her and joking about her speed. I wasn't one of them because I had enough common sense to know how easily it could have been for me to come in last. As I said, I wasn't great at sports.

"Do you know who she is?" Dad asked me. "Do you know her parents?"

I shook my head, "All I know is that she's younger than me."

When the girl did get off the ice, Dad looked around to see if her parents were there. When no one approached her, Dad approached the little girl. With as much enthusiasm as he could muster, he said, "You did such a great job!"

The little girl smiled, her face bright with excitement.

"I think you deserve a treat," Dad added. "Let's go to the canteen."

I didn't know the girl. We weren't friends. She wasn't in my grade. I had seen her before, but I think her family moved away a few years later. I don't remember her name or what she even looked like.

I wonder if she remembers that day or the praise Dad gave her. She may have suppressed the memory, but I haven't forgotten. I remember asking Dad about it a few years after and he couldn't remember because it wasn't a big deal to him – maybe it was just a few kind words and a cheap treat to him, but it made a difference to me.

∞

Another time Dad helped someone was one year near the beginning of summer. This time it was a young man, who was in his mid-thirties. He was hitchhiking across Canada and Tignish was at the top of his bucket list. He loved Stompin' Tom. Dad found this guy when the guy was trying to set up his tent on the beach in Skinner's Pond. Dad was taking a drive with the dog.

"The dog needs a good walk to burn off some energy," he told us before he left.

Mom and I knew it was Dad's code for ice cream. Because Dad was a diabetic and shouldn't have treats, it made them much more desirable. He had a sweet-tooth that no amount of sweets could ever fill. Dad also knew he couldn't bring an ice cream dripping with chocolate sauce in our house without Mom saying something about which leg he wanted cut off.

Dad felt bad for the guy trying to set up his tent. It was still quite cold at night, especially near the beach. The beach was busy, and it wasn't a proper place to try to camp. People were constantly driving ATVs down the shore and the beach was popular at night for beach parties.

"I have a trailer," Dad told him. "It's not much. It's an older camper, but you're welcome to use it for a few days."

The guy agreed, and Dad took him to our house.

Mom and I were getting ready to go to church when they arrived. The guy was one of the tallest people I ever met. He may have needed to crouch just to get into our house. Dad explained to us how he offered the guy a place to stay for a few days. Mom was livid. It was plain to anyone who knew her. Her eyebrows were raised, and her tone of voice changed slightly. No one else would be able to figure out her mood because she was trying to keep it together and be polite but her act wasn't fooling me or Dad. Dad was going to hear it as soon as this guy left.

"I'll get the camper ready after we get back from church," Mom said, politely.

"Your father is crazy," she said, on our way to church.

I sighed. I could hardly believe Dad did that. Dad and I just watched a horror movie about a serial hitchhiker. Didn't he learn anything?

"He is certifiably nuts," Mom muttered under her breath.

At church, I had a new focus for my prayers. *Dear God, please don't let the stranger kill us in our sleep.*

On the drive home from church, we noticed blinking lights.

"Someone's in trouble," Mom said.

The closer we got, the more I realized how close they were to our house.

"Oh my God!" Mom said, her voice sounding anxious when we realized the police car was parked in our yard. "That psycho killed your father."

"Dad didn't even have a fighting chance," I added in.

We were silent when Mom turned in the yard. We weren't yet ready to face whatever was waiting inside.

"Well, let's go in," Mom said, her voice laced with fear.

As we neared the house, we could hear Dad's voice.

"Thank God," Mom said, taking a deep breath.

Dad, the guy, and an RCMP officer were all sitting at the table. The RCMP officer had his notebook out and was busily writing inside. They all looked calm. No one looked out of sorts, or like they had been victims of anything.

"What's going on?" I asked curiously.

"I'll tell you later," Dad promised.

The officer wrote down a few more notes and quietly left. Both Mom and I were anxiously waiting to hear what happened. Our imaginations were running rampant with ideas of what had transpired. Each of these scenarios included the mysterious man Dad brought home.

"Well," Mom prodded. "Are you going to tell us what happened?"

"Some woman related to..." he rambled on, trying to explain who she was. Dad was never good at trying to make the connections.

"Get to the point, Trevor," Mom requested impatiently.

"She was probably going to see our neighbor," Dad explained.

No other words were needed to understand what Dad was talking about for Mom and me but he explained our neighbor to our hitchhiker friend. Our neighbor was an alleged drug dealer. If he didn't peddle drugs, he had a lot of visitors at all times of the day and they only stayed for short visits.

"First thing I know, I see this woman parking her truck in our lane, and the police come blazing in."

"Does this happen a lot?" our hitchhiker friend asked.

"Never!" Dad said.

If our neighbor was dealing drugs, he was good to keep his business on his side of the road. It wasn't an ideal situation, but it could have been worse.

"Thank God, that's all that happened," Mom said, glancing at me. "We got quite a scare when we saw the police in the yard."

"I would have probably been a little scared too if I was in your shoes," our hitchhiker friend confessed. "I am a stranger."

Dad volunteered to take him for a drive to show him some of the pretty sights in our community.

My cousins came to visit when Dad and the hitchhiker were gone. I told them all about our guest staying in the camper. I told them mostly because it was the most interesting thing to happen to us in a while.

"Is she joking, Aunt Lorna?" One cousin asked, wide-eyed.

"I'm afraid not," Mom answered honestly.

"Aren't you afraid that he might kill you guys in your sleep?" My other cousin questioned.

Mom shrugged her shoulders and tried to reassure my cousin and probably herself, "He is only staying in the trailer. We'll make sure the doors are locked tonight."

My cousin's gaze turned toward the backpack in the corner in the living room. It belonged to the hitchhiker.

"What do you think he has in his bag?"

"I'm not sure," Mom answered honestly.

"Maybe we should check," he suggested. "To make sure he doesn't have any weapons."

Mom was leery about our house guest. Still, it seemed wrong to invade his privacy, but it was a major concern that he might try to kill us. A million of ideas of who he could be crossed my mother's mind. Besides being a serial killer, it seemed just as likely that he could be an undercover cop. We all heard stories about their creative undercover identities.

"Maybe we should check," she agreed.

"I'll look," he replied. "You keep watch."

He carefully opened the bag. Inside the bag, they found some clothing and random things useful for camping. Nothing too far-fetched for someone who was hitchhiking across Canada. As my cousin dug further, he noticed a hatchet. A useful tool if you were camping and hitchhiking but could have also been a murder weapon.

"Oh my God, he's going to kill you all," he said.

Mom's heart rate began to rise and the hair prickled on the back of Mom's neck.

"Put it all away!"

Our hitchhiker friend stayed in our camper for a few nights. Our house was locked up securely every night he stayed.

We got to know him a little. He was polite and spoke as if he had been well-educated. To our relief, he was not a serial killer. He didn't make any arrests either, so he probably wasn't an undercover agent. He was just a guy traveling across Canada.

Landon's Journey

"When I saw you I fell in love, and you smiled because you knew."
William Shakespeare

For a little while, when Landon was in high school, Mom, Dad, and I wondered if Landon might have had a calling to the priesthood. Landon never talked about becoming a priest but it was just a feeling that my parents had.

We weren't the only ones who wondered if Landon felt a calling from God to serve as a priest. My grandmother even believed Landon might become a priest. When Landon was younger, the bishop joked with Landon that he would be a priest within ten years and probably a bishop within twenty years.

After Landon dyed his hair blond following the latest trend, some people were convinced that he was the new seminarian. Although he was a teenager, he had the frame of a grown man and had a certain unique maturity that made him appear older.

I guess we wondered because Landon had such a deep spiritual belief in God. When I found it difficult to really focus during the homilies, it came easy for him. He knew answers to hard questions that most people ask about faith and wanted to learn more about our religion. He was the first to raise his hand to take part in retreats and actively took part in the youth group in our church. He read the bible and he could defend his beliefs with strong arguments. He even got into a heated debate about the existence of the Blessed Virgin Mary at school.

He was not perfect by any means. He still could do things that made both Mom and Dad question their parenting abilities. There was just something about him that made both Mom and Dad question if he had been called to serve God through the priesthood.

The idea of Landon becoming a priest was a bit bittersweet to Mom and Dad. They both respected men who devoted their lives to the priesthood and were happy with their religion. Mom came from a strong Catholic family and Dad chose the Catholic religion as an adult. Yet, they weren't sure if it was the path in life they hoped their son would choose.

Dad really had hoped that Landon would continue the family's name. He was the only one of Dad's children who could. My grandfather was one out of two brothers in a family of thirteen children. My great uncle and his wife did not have children, so my grandfather was the only one who continued the Yuill name. Dad feared our branch of the Yuill family might end if Landon were to become a priest.

Mom knew the sacrifices that would need to be made if Landon were to become a priest. It meant he would probably be away from home every Christmas and Easter. If he chose that path, he would not be able to give her grandchildren and instead of sharing him with his new family, his wife and kids, she would have to share him with a whole parish. She also worried that if he became a priest, he would be lonely.

∞

After high school, Landon moved away from home to go to school. He didn't come home every weekend and we didn't hear from him every day, but we knew Landon dated several girls during college. He talked about some of them on the phone or when he was visiting. We even met a few in passing, but the relationships never lasted that long. Landon didn't seem that serious about any of them.

Then he met Amy and everything was different. When he mentioned her name, something changed in his eyes. They sparkled like they never had before. No matter what the conversation was about, somehow it always got turned into something about Amy. We hadn't even met her yet, but we could sense this relationship was different from any other relationship he had ever had. It was the first time we knew for sure Landon wasn't going to go in the direction of the priesthood.

∞

"Mom?" Landon asked as they chatted on the phone one day. He was nervous and Mom feared something was wrong.

"Yeah," she replied.

"That party you're throwing, can I bring Amy?" he asked.

Mom was throwing a vacation-themed party. It was for all their friends and family who weren't going south that year.

"Sure," Mom replied, trying to keep her voice steady. She didn't want him to know how excited she was that Landon was bringing a girl home to introduce to our family and friends.

∞

"She might be the one," Mom told Dad that night. "Amy could be our future daughter-in-law."

"Don't get too excited. We haven't even met her yet," Dad replied, shaking his head. "And besides, don't you think Landon is a little young to be thinking about marriage?"

"He's twenty-one. You were twenty-two when we got married," Mom argued.

∞

On the day of the party, Landon spent the day going over the housework that Mom just did. He washed the windows, cleaned drawers and closets. He put away pictures he didn't like, which included any that he found embarrassing. He warned us all to be on our best behavior as if we had no clue how to behave. Clearly, Landon was nervous.

Amy was everything I hoped my brother would find. She was beautiful, well-spoken, and had enough confidence to go to a party where she only knew one person.

Three days after we met Amy, Landon and Amy broke up. It wasn't a nasty break-up. Amy had just gotten out of a relationship, right before she got into one with Landon, and wanted a little time for herself to figure out what she wanted in life and who she was. The break-up was supposed to last for ten days until Amy could figure out what she wanted but it only lasted two days because she realized what she had with Landon was a good thing.

Landon and Amy developed a strong and emotional relationship very quickly. They had an instant connection and no one doubted that they would end up getting married. From the beginning, they pushed each other to be the best version of themselves that they could be. They made goals that would contribute to a better future for the two of them. But, as strong of a connection they had, they could also get under each other's skin quickly. They were two very determined people. Both were the oldest child in their families and both liked to take charge. They had to work to control their tempers. They could, from time to time, seem to fight often, but usually, the argument would end with the two of them laughing. After one of their fights, Landon called Mom and Dad. It was late at night.

"Amy and I had a big fight," he said. "I'm not sure how to fix it."

"Think before you say something you can't take back," Dad warned.

"You are angry right now so think carefully about what you say and do," Mom urged. "You guys may feel differently when you cool down."

"I don't want to talk about it," Landon replied. "It is what it is. I'll talk to you tomorrow."

"What do you think we should do?" Dad asked Mom.

"Nothing," she said, shaking her head. "We should stay out of it. They'll have to work it out by themselves. We can't fix it for them."

He sighed out of frustration. It clearly wasn't the response from Mom he was hoping for.

"Lorna, they're just kids. They don't know what they are doing and I don't want either of them to make a decision they will regret."

"Trevor, just stay out of it. It's not our place to tell them what to do."

"Okay," he said anxiously.

He waited a few minutes before he climbed out of bed. He was going to do one last check of the fire in the basement before he went to bed, or at least that's what

Mom thought. In reality, he was calling Amy to see what happened and if he could smooth things over for Landon.

"Hello Amy," Dad said, nonchalantly when she answered. Well, as nonchalantly as he could. He had never called Amy before.

"It's a nice night out," he said, trying to make light conversation.

He paused to let her talk before he asked, "Are you having a good night?"

Perhaps not so surprisingly, she told him about the fight she was having with Landon. It was nothing that couldn't be worked out.

Another minute or two passed and I heard Dad saying, "So you guys will be okay?"

"That sounds good," Dad replied. "I'll see you soon."

Landon and Amy ended up getting back together the next day. It wasn't their first fight nor would it be their last but it was the last time Dad got involved. Mom found out, of course, and Mom warned him not to do it again.

∞

Landon and Amy had only been dating a few months when Landon joined the military. For as long as I can remember, Landon always talked about being a police officer and, as it turned out, the military was giving him that chance. It would take a year from the date he enrolled.

Looking back, it was very unexpected that Landon joined the military to become a police officer. He had never really mentioned joining before. He always talked about wanting to live on Prince Edward Island. We thought he would join a police force on the island. Joining the military meant he wouldn't be able to live on the island.

Long distance relationships are not easy, everyone knows that. Landon and Amy were no exceptions to the rule. They missed each other a lot and life was happening for both of them, in two separate spots. Still, though, they were both busy and that helped. Amy was finishing her last year of college and Landon was training hard.

When he was nearing the end of his training, Landon phoned home.

"You'll never believe what I did this weekend."

Mom was silent, waiting for him to continue.

"I bought Amy an engagement ring. I'll bring it next weekend when I come home to show you guys."

"Great!" Mom replied, silently already beginning to prepare for grandchildren. "When are you planning to ask her?"

Landon was unable to disguise the glee in his voice, "On my graduation date! That way it'll be a special day for the both of us."

When he came home the following weekend, in early July, we knew there was a good chance they would be engaged by the end of the weekend. On Friday, he immediately showed Mom, Dad and I, the ring he bought her. Later that evening, before Amy got off from work, he showed Amy's best friend. He showed his friends and almost came close to showing Amy the ring early. He was very excited.

∞

The following day, he admitted he wasn't sure he could wait any longer to propose. Mom played on his vulnerability and urged him to pop the question. She convinced him Amy should have her own special day, free from Landon's graduation. With a little coaxing, he agreed it was the perfect day, much better than waiting until August.

So, with Anne Murray's hit, *Danny's Song* playing in the background, Landon built his confidence up and dropped to his knees. His nerves didn't make it a graceful move to the floor like the movies seem to show it. No. It looked more like he slipped.

An engagement was the last thing Amy expected that day, but what she wanted more than anything. She said, yes!

He still had another two months before he was finished with his training. This time, when he left on Sunday, it wasn't so hard to be apart because they had something exciting to plan and look forward to.

When Landon finished with his training and graduated, he got lucky with his job posting. He was posted to Halifax. It was one of the closest postings to Prince Edward Island. They were both really excited.

Landon and Amy married the following year after they got engaged. It was the same year of Mom and Dad's 25th wedding anniversary. They married on July 10th on one of the hottest and muggiest days of summer. Amy made a beautiful bride and it was a wonderful celebration.

As excited as we were to have Amy officially join our family, it also marked the end of an era. Our family would never be the same again. We were just lucky Amy accepted us as a part of her family, for better or for worse.

Canine Love

"A dog is the only thing on earth that loves you more than he loves himself."

Josh Billings

Some people are cat people and some people are dog people. There are also the people who don't like animals at all. Those are the people who I feel extremely sorry for. Even though they can't see it, they don't know the joy of having a pet keep their feet warm on a cold day or a wet nose nuzzled into your face when you're sad. Nor will these people know what it's like to have an audience every time you sit down to eat a meal.

I'm a dog person. Always have been and always will be. My parents were as well. I can't ever remember a time that we didn't have a dog. A lot of times we had more than one dog, in fact.

∞

The first dog that I ever loved was a dog we rescued. I picked him out when I was three-years-old and his name was Baby. Dad and I were only supposed to be browsing at the animals. Mom and Dad weren't even sure they wanted a dog but there was something special about Baby and we just couldn't leave him behind.

Baby was a Bearded Collie who weighed far below the recommended weight for his breed. His hair was cut short, so short that his skin showed in some spots because of the terrible matting throughout his hair. He was so ugly that he was cute and he was scared of everything. He was gentle and quiet. He lived up to his name, Baby.

The staff at the shelter did not put him in a cage, but they had him by the desk. Before he was rescued by the shelter, he probably didn't have anyone love him and if he did have someone who did love him they weren't very good at it.

Dad knew from the moment I pet Baby that we would not be leaving that shelter without him. He paid the $60, promised that we would get him neutered, and practiced what he was going to tell Mom to make it okay.

Baby quickly became my best-friend. During the day, I spent my time teaching him obedience that he never seemed to learn, building forts, and going on picnics. He was my company. I didn't feel as alone during the mornings when Dad was having his tube feedings. At night time, he slept at the foot of my bed.

He barked when people came to the door and from the sound of his bark he sounded vicious, or in the very least – courageous, but Baby wasn't. He would hide behind my parents whenever anyone came over until he was sure that the visitors were safe for him to approach.

The broom terrified him and he would often go to a bedroom until we were done sweeping. He hated it when voices were raised and did his best to soothe it over. He would nuzzle his nose under an arm to urge someone to pet him or he clacked his teeth together to resemble a smile.

He was kind and patient. He let me dress him in clothing and put pony tails in his hair, but he was not perfect. Although he never played with chew toys, he couldn't resist chewing the odd doll or action figure. He tore every garbage bag apart, but I couldn't really blame him. After all, we learned that he was locked in a shed with only garbage to eat before he came to live with us.

We had Baby for thirteen years when old age was getting the best of him. He didn't sleep on the warm beds but preferred the living room. He didn't see as well and ran into walls. He didn't come when we called him and he didn't budge when there were loud noises.

"Can we get another dog?" I asked Mom and Dad. "This time a puppy. He might get Baby off the floor with his energy."

"We are a one dog kind of family," Dad replied.

∞

Finally, one night I heard Mom relent.

"Trevor?" I heard her say, long after she assumed I was probably asleep.

Secrets or private discussions didn't exist in our house. There was no privacy. Our open multi-level concept home had a unique design that gave our family plenty of room but its downfall – a conversation upstairs could be heard downstairs. The only time Mom and Dad could have private conversations was if we weren't home or if we were really asleep.

"I think we should get another dog," she told him.

"Are you crazy?" I heard Dad ask her. "We already have a dog."

"Baby is old and he will not live forever," she reasoned. "Another dog will soften the blow for Atara."

"Lorna, she needs to learn to grieve someday."

"You're right. Someday she will have to learn to grieve and there will be nothing we can do to make it better," Mom continued, "but if we can do something now to help her, let's do it."

"Okay," Dad agreed.

∞

I had the difficult task the next day of pretending I didn't know we were getting another dog! That is a tough secret to keep, believe me! All I wanted to do was jump in glee and check the classifieds.

Two days later, the day before my exams started, Dad came to school during second period. He told me he had a paper that Mom needed me to sign out in the car.

DID I TAKE THE WRONG ROAD?

In the car was the smallest dog I had ever seen. He was part Lhasa-Apso and part Toy Poodle. He looked like a teddy bear and it took all my might to walk back inside that school and go back to class.

I named him Zack. It took some time to adjust to a puppy. He had so much energy and we weren't use to it. Baby's idea of being energetic was walking to his food dish and, on a good day, to the top of the stairs.

The new puppy was into everything. Nothing was safe from Zack's destruction, but he did seem to bring a little life back to Baby, who would try to join in now and then.

∞

One day before Christmas, when the school break was just beginning, I was cleaning downstairs. Zack was playing with a stuffed toy when I left him alone for one minute.

That one minute was just long enough to hear a loud crash! My dog, who weighed less than ten pounds, had knocked the Christmas tree right out of its stand. Immediately, he was playing with the white beads Mom had hung on the tree. In seconds it seemed, he had the white beads all knotted up. You can imagine how excited Mom and Dad were.

∞

It was the first year we were using an artificial Christmas tree. Mom and Landon loved the smell and the fullness of a real Christmas tree. Dad and I hated the mess of pine needles that could still be found throughout January. Dad and I had use a lot of persuasion that year to get Mom and Landon to agree to a fake tree. In early December, the four of us went to the store, determined to pick just the right Christmas tree. We picked the fake tree out and bought it, it came in a box. We took home the box and the pine candle that we had bought. However, when we took the tree out of the box, all of us seemed surprised. The tree looked nothing like the tree on the box. It had gaps between the branches and wasn't the thick tree in the store – it was made of wire and whatever else and looked that way. Frankly, it didn't quite look like a tree – certainly, not a real one.

"I told you an artificial tree was not as good as a real tree," Mom said, as we finished fluffing the last branch on the tree. "I'll make it work for this year but never again."

Mom did her best. The tree had the best of the decorations that we could find and the gaps were filled in. She made the fake tree resemble what a Christmas tree *should* look like, but in less than a minute, Zack had done his damage.

Zack didn't listen well. He didn't come when you called his name. He wasn't afraid to chew things and he ran outside the minute that the door opened enough for him to get out.

One afternoon he had gotten outside. It was freezing rain outside that day. Dad and I called for him while we put on our boots. In fact, we hadn't even gotten our boots on when he was hit by a car. He died instantly.

I was devastated. Dad was devastated. Mom hadn't bonded with Zack, but she was devastated more so because we were devastated.

That night, again when Dad thought that I was asleep, he asked Mom. "Do we have enough money in the account to get a dog?"

"If we want to be strapped this month then, yes," she answered. "I think we can swing it, if you think we need to."

"We need to swing it," he responded.

The next day, Dad picked me up early from school. He refused to tell me why we were going to Charlottetown, a two hour trip, before a major storm was coming.

∞

Jackson was our next dog. He was a four-month-old Shih-Tzu mix and he had to be re-homed as the result of a well-gestured, but poorly received gift to a grandmother.

If we thought Zack was a bad dog, Jackson was the worst dog that ever existed. Jackson only listened to Dad and, even then, only if he wanted to. He was very attached to Dad and would yelp when Dad wasn't home. It was easy to understand his attachment to Dad because Dad was home with him a lot and cooked him a breakfast of eggs and toast every morning.

Jackson destroyed everything. Our house had more gates than a brand-new childproof house and yet he still wrecked things. We wanted to wring his neck most of the time.

∞

"Can you go to my house and get my coat?" Nena asked Dad one day. Since Papa passed away, Nena went to my aunts' houses in Ontario for the winter. "I'd like you to mail it to me."

"Which one?" Dad asked.

"It's red," she responded. "The one your father had made specifically for me. It has the fur on the hood."

"Okay," Dad replied.

The next day, Dad went to Nena's and found her coat. He brought it to our house so he could get it ready for the mail. He set it on the couch and he made supper.

"Where's Jackson?" Mom asked, aware that if Jackson was quiet there was a good chance – it meant he was doing something he shouldn't be.

"Jackson?" Dad called.

Jackson came trotting in with his mouth full.

"What does he have in his mouth?" Dad asked.

Mom pulled Jackson close and opened his mouth.

"We're in trouble," she announced in a panicked tone.

Dad looked at her hand and the fur from Nena's custom-made coat.

"What are we going to do? We're as good as dead."

Mom held the clump of fur in her hand.

"What do I do with it?"

"Put it in the pocket of the coat for now," he told her.

Mom stuffed the fur in the pocket, "She's going to kill us."

"Is there any way we can fix it?" Dad asked.

Mom looked at the coat and felt pressured because she knew how much the coat meant to Nena.

"Let's take it somewhere and see."

The next day, Mom brought it to a local guy who could fix just about anything. Tents, leather, upholstery.

"Please," Mom begged, "You gotta fix it. It'll start a family feud if you can't."

"I'll do the best I can so no one can notice," he promised.

To buy some time, Dad called Nena, "I guess I don't have the right address. Your coat came back in the mail. The address is apparently undeliverable."

Nena gave the address again.

"I'll put it in the mail the first chance I get," he promised her.

A little more than a week later and the coat was ready to go. Fur was missing so the only way he could fix it was by taking a small piece out of the hood. The change was hard to spot.

"Thank God," Dad said, as he saw the coat. "That's a secret we take to the grave."

Jackson was a good exercise program. He loved escaping the house and running. His electric shock collar fence seemed to be broken more than it worked. It didn't work if too much snow was covering the wires and the collar ate through batteries.

Running was a game for Jackson. He would check to see if we were watching what he was doing while he was running. He gained extra points if he could get out when you were already late for something. More than once, he had traffic on the Western Road stopped as he darted through the stopped cars.

I was 18 when Dad landed in the hospital in Moncton. It was unexpected and we weren't prepared.

"What are we going to do with the dog?" I asked Mom. "Could we ask Nena to take him?"

"No," she said. "He would have her running all through O'Leary. We'll take his cage and take him with us. He can stay at the hotel in his cage while we visit your father."

"Okay," I agreed.

Landon and Amy met us in Moncton. We were sharing a hotel room.

The next morning, Landon held the door open, just a crack to ask Amy to grab him something from their car because she was there. The small crack was just big enough for Jackson to escape.

The hotel was on the highway and it took Jackson about two seconds to reach the highway. He made it across four lanes of busy traffic. Landon, Amy, Mom, and I chased after him. Amy and I were both in our pajamas.

He ran to a grocery store. We hoped he would go in because it would be easy to trap him but he wasn't heavy enough to sensor the automatic doors to open. Instead, he went to the office supply store next. Again, the doors would not open. He ran to the highway again.

A bus driver stopped at the lights and took sympathy on us. He opened his doors and yelled, "Here poochie, poochie."

Jackson appeared interested and got close enough to the bus that we thought our game was over. I breathed a sigh of relief. The relief was short-lived as Jackson ran away from the bus.

For over an hour, we chased Jackson as he ran through the highway and down residential streets. We followed him through yards and private property as Jackson kept running and playing his game.

"How attached are you to this dog?" Landon asked, "I'll buy you a new dog."

"We're not leaving him behind," I said firmly.

We came close several times to catching him. He would let us get close enough to him to almost grab him and then he would take off again, it was part of his game.

"We got him cornered," Landon finally said, as we all came closer to him than we had before.

"He's going your way, Mom," I said.

We watched as Jackson quickly went through her legs. She didn't even come close to catching him.

As frustrated as we were, we kept running after him. We tried reverse psychology and going in the opposite direction but Jackson didn't catch on or he didn't care. He kept running.

The only reason we caught him was because he got stuck in a fence. Landon firmly grabbed him and held him close as we walked back to our hotel. Jackson was quickly put in his cage.

After that was over, Mom and I drove to the hospital. Landon and Amy brought Jackson to a dog kennel in the area, not wanting a repeat of the morning.

"Don't tell your father about Jackson," Mom warned. "Your father has enough on his plate without worrying about the dog."

"Okay," I said, "You'll have to warn Landon and Amy."

Before we even had a chance to tell Landon, the first thing he said was, "I can't believe we chased that white dog all across Moncton."

A Hard-Working Man

"You never fail until you stop trying."
Albert Einstein

When I was in elementary school, I quickly discovered there was something different about Dad than all my classmates' fathers. It wasn't all the trips we made to the hospital or even the abundance of medical supplies in my parents' bedroom. It was the fact that I had no idea what Dad did for a job.

Dad worked on tractors sometimes but it wasn't really a job. He didn't do it every day so I wasn't convinced it was his profession.

Determined to find out what Dad's job was, I asked Mom, "What does Dad do?"

She looked confused, "What do you mean?"

"The kids in my class," I explained, "all their fathers have jobs. A lot of them fish and a few are carpenters. They all seem to go to work but I'm not sure what Dad does."

She hummed, unsure how to answer, "Remember how I told you that Dad was in an accident before you were born?"

I nodded.

"Well before he got hurt, he worked on vehicles and tractors," she explained, "but since he got hurt, he can't do that anymore."

"So, Dad doesn't work?" I asked.

"He works very hard," she replied. "He cooks supper every night and he fixes everything around here. He just can't work on cars and big trucks anymore. He can only work on smaller things."

"Like bicycles?" I asked.

"That's right," she answered.

And that is the reason why I believed for several years that Dad was a bicycle mechanic.

∞

A few years had passed and I was in junior high. I no longer believed Dad was a bicycle mechanic. "I'm going to work tomorrow," Dad told us as we ate our supper one evening.

"You're going to work?" Mom asked surprised. "Where?"

"I'm going to drive a truck and haul potatoes," Dad replied.

"Are you serious?" Mom asked.

"Yes," he answered.

"Alright!" I replied, already envisioning the new wardrobe I would buy with Dad's salary.

"Do you think you're going to be able to work?" Mom asked.

"I hope so," Dad replied.

The next day, after a hard day at work, it was clear Dad was not going to be able to work. His body was still recovering from his broken neck injury that had only occurred a few years prior. He didn't have the necessary strength to work a full-time job. He needed a job that allowed him to work when he felt able to and at his own pace.

"Don't sweat it," Mom told him. "It would have been nice if it would have worked out but we'll manage. We always do."

∞

A few more years had passed and I was in college. Dad was stronger than I had ever seen him before.

"I think I'm ready to go back to work," Dad announced.

"Okay," Mom said.

Dad's new working career began by taking a career exploration course. Mom was trying to encourage Dad to find a job that would be easier on his body, but being a mechanic was all Dad ever knew. He didn't know what else he could do.

I always believed Dad was one of the smartest people I've ever met. Dad, who despite the fact he didn't go on the internet for many years, was able to fix the family computer. He knew how to fix just about any appliance in the house. Whenever I needed help, Dad was the first one I went to.

The career exploration program was a good opportunity for him. He learned a lot about himself, gained some work experience and he developed a working routine. While it was good for him mentally, unfortunately, it just didn't lead to any jobs.

Eventually, however, he got a job maintaining the shore. It was a work project so from the start it was understood that the job wouldn't last forever but, it was a step in the right direction. He cleaned the road leading to the shore, removing any litter. He maintained any of the signs and did the necessary upkeep near the shore. After the project ended, Dad was getting close to earning enough of an annual income that he would no longer be eligible for his disability amount.

"What do you want to do, Trevor?" Mom asked. "We worked too hard to let it go. It's not much but it's a help if you get really sick again."

"I like working," Dad said. "I'm going to see if there is anything they can do for me."

We were never very lucky at catching breaks but that was one break that worked for us. Dad was able to keep his disability support going while he worked.

Dad was determined he was going to find another job. When he did find another job, it was another short-term job working for a hardware store. Out of all the work experiences Dad had since his accident, I think the hardware store was one of his favorites. He enjoyed the work and he happily anticipated getting up every morning and going to work there.

It was also one of the only jobs where he worked constantly with other people and he enjoyed it. He was proud when they gave him a uniform shirt because that made him a part of their team.

∞

After that project, Dad found another job as a carpenter's helper. Mom and I feared it wasn't the job for him. As talented as Dad was in so many different skills, carpentry was not one of them. If Dad had the hammer out both of us feared what he was trying to fix or build. Often, Dad would have a pencil behind his ear, take three days to come up with the plan, and we would end up with something that served its purpose but was ugly and rough around the edges.

The work was harder than the other jobs. He did the best he could but the work was taking its toll on his health. Dad came home tired, cold, and his body was aching.

"You don't have to keep working there," Mom reminded him several times.

"It's okay," Dad replied. "The others help me, so it's not that bad."

Dad was lucky. His co-workers often helped him and Dad didn't have to carry the heavy equipment or supplies. Some would encourage him to take breaks when he could so he would be able to continue working.

∞

One of the last jobs Dad worked before his health declined to the point where he was no longer able to work, was at the same health centre where Mom worked. He also enjoyed his work there. He did any maintenance work that needed to be done. Dad enjoyed the responsibility and respect he was given there. Any ideas he suggested were always well received and given the necessary attention.

I respected my father for working and doing what he could, despite his circumstances.

Career Choices

"If you do what you love, you'll never work a day in your life."

Marc Anthony

Unlike my brother, who always had a good idea of what he wanted to do, I never knew. I changed my mind dozens of times, starting from the time I was five-years-old. I wanted to be a taxi cab driver. I thought they had the best job ever. They got to sit in a car all day long and meet all kinds of interesting people. I remember sitting in Mom and Dad's car and practicing my steering abilities all morning long. Sometimes I would move all the towels underneath the vanity upstairs and I pretended it was a van with my teddy bears as passengers. It didn't take long before I changed my mind of becoming a taxi driver.

Throughout the years, I wanted to become a doctor, an ophthalmologist, a veterinarian, an X-Ray technician, a computer technician, a pilot, a chef, and a lawyer. I'm sure there were a few other occupations that I thought I might like to do as well.

For a long time, I wanted to be a teacher, like my grandmother on my mother's side and my great-grandmother on my father's side. I taught religion classes for community bursary hours when I was in high school and I think I could have easily envisioned myself preparing lesson plans and teaching. I liked school supplies and I still enjoy the back-to-school sales. However, when I graduated high school, it seemed like there were more teachers than teaching jobs. It would be a waste of a time to gain a degree in a field that did not need any more professionals.

I was accepted to both university and college. I ended up at college for a career that was not for me. It was extremely frustrating because I wanted it to work. I wanted to like the career choice because there were jobs available in that field.

I found my calling in the helping field, through a summer job. I knew that my heart belonged in the human services field. I immensely enjoyed that summer and I learned a lot about myself, the human spirit, and how to better connect with people. I wasn't sure how to enter the field. I was questioning whether I should enroll into university when, by accident, I found an advertisement for a French college.

I knew little about the college or even what programs they offered. All I knew was that they had the most annoying commercial on the radio, the type sure to get stuck in your head. I looked into the college and it was a great option. It was close to home.

I was worried about completing a program in a second language. It seemed a little daunting. In high school, French immersion students took one seventy-minute course each semester, either a French class or a social studies course. All of the other courses were in English. What would it be like to study entirely in a different language?

"Take a leap of faith," Mom suggested. "You can do anything you set your mind to."

"Except become a Catholic priest," Dad joked.

I enrolled at the college, not really knowing what to expect and I anxiously waited for September to arrive. All summer long I attempted to work on my knowledge of the French language. I tried to remember all the French words I had forgotten.

The first day of college finally came. My stomach was full of butterflies and my brain was mixed with a variety of English and French words creating a unique Franglais dictionary. I was terrified that I was going to forget how to say my first name in French which I hate the way my name sounds in French. Some people are so lucky - their already perfect-sounding English name translates into an even prettier exotic version in French. Well, not me. My name finishes with the sound of a rat in French.

I was one of the last people to arrive for the orientation that morning and I was pleasantly surprised by the number of people in the room. There were about twelve students or so. There were some people who were younger, some that graduated the same time I did, and some who were older. It was a perfect blend and enough students that it would hopefully invite meaningful relaxed discussions. I would have preferred if I didn't have to join in every discussion but instead could listen keenly.

As the morning progressed, I quickly learned that these were not just the students in my program like I originally believed, but these were all the first-year students in the entire college. Only about twelve students! Each student took the time to introduce themselves and the program they were enrolled in; I made the observation that I was the only one enrolled in my program. What did I get myself into?

"How do you think you'll do?" Dad asked me that night.

"Well Dad, I have a really good feeling that I am going to be at the top of my class. I may even be valedictorian for my program." I boasted.

The college was pretty resourceful and knew how to save money when it was possible. Some of the courses that I needed to take were not required to be taken in a particular sequence and I could join the second-year students, which brought the total class size to four students. Other courses were taken in the evening with people who were required to upgrade in order to be grandfathered into their current government job. There was only a handful of my courses that I was the only student.

My first college hurdle was to learn the name of my program. Human Services sounds easy enough, but the French translation is a little harder. Intervenant en Service à la Personne contained many more syllables.

It was a great experience. The small class sizes made my education more intimate and some of the lesson plans were centered on my specific needs. Class times even changed to accommodate a student who was going away for a week. The small class sizes forced me to come out of my comfort zone. With such small classes, you had no choice but to take an active role in class discussions.

I am proud that I could complete a postsecondary education in French. My maternal grandparents were Acadian French and Mom remembers when she was young, they spoke mostly in French at home. In fact, she remembers going to a religion class in English and she struggled to understand what they were saying. As she grew older, they spoke less and less French and spoke English as their dominant language. Now, Mom can speak only a few words in French although her French comprehension is much better. In some weird way, going to a French college made me feel connected with my heritage.

A woman who had completed her first year several years earlier joined me in the second year and there were several people in the first year of the Human Services program.

Almost two years later after a few on-the-job training experiences, many nights of hard studying, and a better comprehension of French grammar (but still not even close to perfection) and I was ready to graduate and join the workforce. The French graduation ceremony with my Anglophone family was interesting, however, like I promised- I ended up as valedictorian.

The problem after graduation was that I could not find a job in my field. A few months before I graduated I found a job at a call center. It was okay but yet another reason I was glad that I was going to have an education. I was not one who fared well in a customer service job. Because of confidentiality reasons, we took calls from the other side of the country, usually from the large cities. The majority of the calls that I dealt with were from people who were wondering why their bills were ridiculously high. My job, whether I believed the charges were just or not, was usually to claim that the charges were legit. Most of the customers were not happy and grateful. There were customers who had bills that toppled over a thousand dollars or even more. Sometimes the charges were valid, but there were other times that I felt sympathy for the customers who were paying because their child accidentally went over data.

What made the job even more challenging was that a lot of the callers did not speak English as their first language. Their language was broken and difficult to understand. Since you are talking on the phone, you can't even take advantage of nonverbal communication. I wasn't good at understanding broken English and I spent half of my time asking customers to repeat what they were saying. Some probably believed that I was hired through some inclusive policy.

I couldn't wait to quit that job and find work in my studied field. The problem was that there was no work. I expected when I was finished with school that the job offers would pile in and I would find work with no issues. The only notice I received after I graduated was from the Student Loan office reminding me that in six short months, I would be making payments on a loan that would take me forever to pay back.

Deciding I was going to make my mark in my field one way or another, I searched the job bank daily and applied to every single job that was remotely related to my field, whether I believed I had a shot of attaining the job or not. I also dropped off my portfolio to every organization I knew.

The majority of the places where I dropped my portfolios were not hiring so I didn't get a lot of calls. I went through orientation for two different jobs and I was put on their relief list. I think one place put me through orientation just so I would stop calling them. The relief list was one step closer to gaining employment. It would be my first paid experience in the field.

At the beginning of July, I finally got a job. The job was working with a young guy who had autism. He had an annual sum of money to spend on having a worker for social skill building and tutoring. As excited as I was with the full weeks' workload during the summer, it didn't change the fact that he started school again in September – I wouldn't have as many hours and he wouldn't have as much funding to keep me on the books.

Being on a relief list is a lot like being a gambler. Each week you pray to the good Lord that you will get enough work. If you do accept work and it is only a small shift, you feel discouraged when someone calls and you had to decline a shift that was double the length. You never quite know how your day will turn out. You may expect that you have no work, but in a matter of minutes, you get ready for a day of work and an evening of work somewhere else. The life of a relief worker is not for everyone. It requires a certain amount of flexibility. Some of the relief shifts don't even make economic sense. I have accepted split shifts in the past, which is another difficult work shift. It starts early in the morning and lasted for three hours before I was given an eight-hour break and then went back to work for five hours that evening. The eight hours off in the middle wasn't enough time to travel back home, so I stayed in town to window shop.

Window shopping is never *just* window shopping. There is always something that you see that you just cannot leave behind. You convince yourself that if you don't buy it that very moment you will never get another chance to buy it again and it'll be the worst mistake you've ever made and the world will fall apart. I hate that feeling of guilt when I leave a store empty-handed. I've done nothing wrong but yet as I leave the store empty-handed, for whatever reason, I convince myself that I need to act innocent. I sometimes even try to rush out of the store before the cashier tells me to have a nice day. I feel that if they don't think that I am shoplifting, then they must believe that I am an intolerable customer. When I finally am outside of the store, I breathe a sigh of relief and it feels kind of like I just pulled off the great Canadian crime. Silly, I know.

So, I did the split shift for two days in a row and I successfully spent more money than what I earned for those two days. I had to rethink my purpose. One year after graduating from college, I still had no job guaranteeing any amount of hours each week. Over the winter, I was lucky enough to find 21 hours a week - three hours seven days a week for about three months. I was grateful for the work. It was near my home and I could still pick up relief hours. It did, however, lead to my name being taken off the relief list at the other organization. The thing about relief work is that if you say no one time too many, they stop calling you.

That summer was busy. I continued to work with the young guy who had autism. I worked two and a half days doing one-on-one work with the young man and I did relief shifts when I could. I was happy with the work over the summer, but I feared, like I had the summer before, that September would be slow. People would run out of vacation time and try to save enough time for the holidays and my hours, doing one-on-one work, could easily have been taken away.

I was beginning to despair that I would never have a full-time job. I knew I loved the field but I also worried that there was no real way to advance in my field – to even really find a career in my field - and it would be a long time until retirement. I wanted to feel like I was working towards something that would give me more of an edge in the workforce, so I looked into educational options. The college I had graduated from and a university had recently signed an articulation agreement where my degree counted two years towards another degree and it seemed ideal for me.

I traveled to Charlottetown two nights a week for psychology and anthropology courses. I got along really well and enrolled as a full-time student for the winter semester. I was also encouraged to go to school full-time because Dad had a disability. If I went full-time, I would be entitled to a small amount each month to help cover the cost of classes.

I enjoy learning and I even enjoy the challenges that come with learning. One course I took was psychopharmacology. Psychopharmacology has probably aged me before my time. The first time that I opened the book, I cried and didn't open it for at least a month. The guidelines suggested that students needed adequate knowledge of the human brain and body which meant something different for me than it did to the other students. I had struggled academically, I felt overwhelmed. I could only read short paragraphs and, even then I required a break to wrap my mind around what I had just read. Amazingly, I passed the course and, due to that, I tell myself I can accomplish any feat.

Hellos and Good-Byes

"The family is one of nature's masterpieces."
George Santayana

For as long as I can remember, Dad lived his life with the expectation he would die soon. It didn't make him sad. He stated it enough that it didn't even make us sad. It was just a fact. The sky is blue. Fact. Albert Einstein was a genius. Fact. Trevor Yuill is going to die. Fact.

My young ignorance protected me from understanding. Ignorance isn't even the correct term to use. He said it so much that the words no longer had meaning. Hearing the words kind of felt like reading a tabloid magazine. According to them, the world should have ended at least once a year.

"I won't make it to thirty-five," Dad would say.

But Dad turned thirty-five. So, on his thirty-fifth birthday, he vowed, "I'll not make it to forty."

Yet again he turned forty. It wasn't the best way to celebrate a fortieth birthday. As previously mentioned a bit earlier on, Dad was in the hospital in Moncton. He was in traction with weights attached to his head. We celebrated with one piece of cake found by a team of thoughtful nurses. They also brought us meal trays from discharged patients so we could enjoy our meal together. It was the first meal we had eaten together in weeks. It may not have been the best way to celebrate, but he made it to 40.

Then he stopped using numbers. He started to count his life by the events he didn't figure he would be around for. The one that he talked about the most was not being around for the birth of any of his grandchildren.

When Dad would talk about dying, I would roll my eyes. We heard it too often and Dad continued to amaze us. I secretly wondered if Dad would outlive us all.

In 2012, when Dad was forty-nine years old, his first grandchild was born. Benjamin Eli Leonard Yuill weighed over ten pounds. He had ten fingers and ten toes and he was perfect in every way. His difficult birth made him a force to be reckoned with. As Dad held Ben for the first time in the Neo-Natal Unit, he smiled proudly.

"I never thought I would see the day where I would meet my grandchild."

Only a few days after Ben was born, Dad was admitted to the hospital with extreme pain in his abdomen. He was having a pancreatitis attack. It was the first one he had in years and it was really taking its toll on him. He was in the hospital for about a month, the longest I ever remember him being in the hospital.

Things changed when Dad came home from the hospital. They didn't change overnight but rather gradually and with no one understanding what was happening. Looking back, Ben's birth seemed to be the catalyst to his poor health. It was like his mission, everything he wanted to accomplish on his bucket list before he died, was complete. His body was tired and he had enough. He had seen his first grandson and knew the Yuill name would continue.

In February, he was admitted to Prince County Hospital in Summerside. He was in a lot of pain, his blood panel was all out of whack, and he was constantly throwing up. He thought for sure he was having another pancreatitis attack. There were more things wrong with his blood panel than what was right but he wasn't having another pancreas attack. He had an infection in his blood. He was losing a lot of weight around that time and he barely marked a hundred pounds. He couldn't afford to lose any more weight, but his stomach was no longer allowing him to digest most food. Another issue he was constantly dealing with were his blood sugars. His blood sugars would range from a low to a high in a matter of an hour or vice versa. To make matters worse, his body was so accustomed to having such a variety of different blood sugars that Dad no longer showed symptoms of a high or a low. He could talk to a nurse with a blood sugar of 2.4 mmol, acting not at all bothered when most people would feel the anxiety, hunger, nausea, weakness, lightheadedness or the difficulty in concentrating that was associated with low blood sugar.

He was admitted to the hospital off and on for the years that followed Ben's birth. One medical issue would get cleared up and he would be confronted by another problem. Dad's resilience was no longer there.

When he was in the hospital, Mom and I would do our best to visit him every day.

"How are you feeling today, Dad?" I would ask every time I visited.

"So-so," he would always respond.

'So-so' was Dad's catchphrase and every time I heard him say it, I would cringe. It was the most annoying answer ever because it was hard to decipher how he really felt. Was he on the road to recovery or was he getting worse?

Besides the pain that still lingered with him, caused by the trauma of the accident, he was also experiencing a lot of pain because he developed gastroparesis. Years of constant high blood sugars had caused his nerves to become damaged. The muscles in his stomach weren't working like they were supposed to. His stomach could not fully and normally empty itself. To add to his misery, there was extensive scar tissue in his stomach because of all the surgeries and procedures.

Drugs didn't really help control the pain. His stomach hurt for so many years that he had developed a tolerance to the medication and they no longer effectively helped with pain control. It was tough to find a balance of a dosage that was somewhat effective but still safe. Decades of pain pills meant that he built a tolerance to them and needed a lot of medication to make a difference. He had developed a tolerance that bordered on a level that was unsafe.

It was clear that he was in a lot of pain. His pain never diminished. The pain only increased and that made him terrified. The drugs turned him into a person he didn't like. He depended completely on the nurses at the hospital. He kept a constant watch on the time. At home, the medications were all there. He had access to all of it. He knew exactly how long they had to last and the consequences if they didn't last that long. At the hospital, he didn't have any control. If the nurses were running a half hour later with the medications or longer, then he was at their mercy.

Dad was terrified of pain. He lived his life to avoid any unnecessary pain. He restricted his movements and did most of his work, like going for walks, based on when the pain pills would be the most effective.

There were a few of the nurses who were not very sympathetic. It left you to wonder how they could possibly work in such a position which required a strong sense of empathy and sympathy. They neglected to see him as the person he was: a father, a husband, a son, a brother, and a grandfather. He might not have been important to them, but he was someone who was loved very much. He was not just the patient who only rang the buzzer when his pain medications were due. Not all the nurses were like that. Some of the nurses went the extra mile. They made him feel important and that his needs were a priority.

One nurse, in particular, went the extra mile for Dad. One day, when Dad was having an extremely hard day, she sat down with him and she listened as he talked about how he had too much to do at home to be sick. She listened knowing there wasn't much that she could do besides listen.

From my perspective, it didn't seem like the doctors who were in charge of Dad's care always knew what they should do either. He wasn't a textbook case. No studies were done because there weren't any identical cases. At one of the hospitals where he was admitted, a family doctor was assigned to the patients on the floor. Each week the doctor changed, which sometimes was a good thing and sometimes it was a bad thing. A new doctor could bring a different perspective with new ideas, knowledge, and a whole new plan. On the other hand, a different doctor could be frustrating. They had plenty of ideas of how Dad should be treated. They changed things but would only be around just long enough to start the new plan and not follow through. So, the plans for his care often changed. It was tough when there was a medication change. Dad felt a lot of side effects from many of the medications and very few of them actually helped. It made him hesitant to want to try any other medication changes.

Dad had worse days when we weren't able to visit him. Work still had to be done. The grass still needed to be cut in the summer with a lawnmower that had seen its better days. The house still needed to be cleaned. Dad's admission to the hospital didn't stop the snow from falling. Life still continued.

The first winter Dad spent in the hospital was the most difficult. We weren't really prepared. He was brought to the hospital in February by ambulance and he didn't come home until summer.

The house was equipped for Dad and no one else. Without training from Dad, we were going to be lost. No manual could explain how to operate Dad's upgraded features. His instructions, from the bedside, to change the heat from wood to oil, included "listen to the pipe that makes the noise" and "turn that pipe but be careful not to touch the others" was really no help. It just made us certain we were not going to the basement.

Not wanting Dad to worry about us, we would always respond the same way, "We'll be fine."

I was lucky to have gained three hours of temporary work, every day. Picking up the occasional shift besides the temporary work gave me enough work and I no longer had to accept shifts further away from home.

After working three hours in the morning, if I had no other work for the day, I drove to Summerside to visit Dad. After visiting for near five hours, I would go home. Mom and I would make something quick for supper and then we would pray that the fire would light easily.

No matter how hard we ever tried, the fire never lit easily. We would dip paper lightly in cooking oil, pray it would light but the cooking oil only gave it a big start and then it would die out.

We had to resort to bringing a cot for me to sleep on in Mom and Dad's room. We would warm the closed room with a small space heater. It was the only way we could feel a little warmth in the house.

By the time the fire started to circulate heat throughout the house, it was time for bed. The house never actually warmed up enough to be comfortable. Between an infrared heater, the small space heater, and a late-night fire, it still seemed cold and we had to just hope, that with a little luck, the pipes didn't freeze. We must have had angels looking out for us.

The bedroom was our solace. It was the only room warm enough to take our coats off in. The room provided temporary relief from the cold. The rest of the house was so cold that I remember limiting what I was drinking because I didn't want to leave the room to go to the bathroom until morning.

One winter night, after another failed attempt at a fire, in a fit of frustration, Mom threw a pair of old jeans into the fire. The wood stove, seemingly appreciative of our sacrifice, started a nice fire. Every winter night after that evening we would begrudgingly look through closets to find a pair of jeans we were willing to sacrifice. I ended up losing quite a few pairs of jeans that winter. We didn't dare tell Dad because he certainly would not have approved. He would have complained that it was bad for the stove. Bad for the stove or not, we didn't care. We wanted heat.

For years, I lived a life of luxury, especially in the winter. Dad was small and liked the heat. He was home all the time, so his job was to make the house as hot as possible. He stoked the fire late at night and in the wee hours of the morning. The fire never went out at our house. While the wind blew the snow around outside and the temperatures dipped far below the freezing point, I was inside comfortably lounging in my t-shirt and shorts, which I wore as pajamas despite the cold season. I wasn't used to being cold.

∞

In March of 2015, my niece Hallie was born. She made the perfect addition to our little family. Landon had the million-dollar family. They had a boy and now they had a girl.

We couldn't be there when Hallie was born. Dad was still in the hospital and he was having a procedure done around the same time. Mom and I didn't want to leave him behind.

We met Hallie a few weeks after, on their visit after she was born on the island. It was a different experience with Hallie than it was with Ben. With Ben, it was such a different feeling. It felt like our family changed instantly. He was the first baby born in our immediate family, the start of the new generation of Yuill's and the first baby born on Mom's side of the family in a long time. Ben changed our family and it was changed for the better, but his birth sparked a change. Family meals had to be changed to accommodate children.

On the other hand, it felt like Hallie was always a part of our family. There was no adjustment period. She just fit well into our family. I couldn't imagine what our family would feel like again without her. My father got to meet his second grandchild.

∞

It was only a few weeks after Hallie was born when Landon had to leave for training for his deployment. He was fairly lucky up to that point. He had never been deployed, which was every mother's dream, but the guilt of not being deployed was getting to Landon. A lot of the people he worked with and knew in the military had gone on at least one deployment. Well, it was his turn.

Protecting the rights of the innocent and making the world a little safer were the main reasons that Landon had signed up – and, of course, he wanted to be a military officer. He had, however, signed up for the military before he had kids and he hadn't expected it would be so hard to leave them behind.

Obviously, the timing was a little less than ideal for Landon to be away from home. A newborn baby and a two-year-old was a tall order for anyone, but with Landon away, it was just harder. What made it a little worse was that Landon and Amy lived in Middleton,

Nova Scotia. Middleton was six hours away and they had no family nearby who could help Amy out when she needed it when Landon was gone.

Around the same time as Landon was preparing to leave, the doctors realized that Dad's health was more than what they could treat on the island and they referred him to a gastrointestinal specialist at the Victoria General Hospital in Halifax. He just had to wait until a bed became available.

The day that a bed became available was the same day that Landon and Amy were leaving to go back to their home in Nova Scotia because Landon was deploying the following day. Both Landon and Dad were off to fight their own individual battles.

Mom and I couldn't go with Dad. He was leaving to go to the Queen Victoria General on a Sunday and we both had to work the following day. Had it been an emergency, we could have, but in that scenario, it wasn't. Neither of us could have afforded to take a temporary leave of absence. I didn't even have a job to take a leave of absence from. It was only casual work, a temporary position.

The following weekend we traveled to Halifax. Between Mom and me, I was the only one who could drive. Mom wasn't a very good driver of standard transmission cars. She stalled often and lost her patience quick. I had never driven in Halifax before so it was bound to be an interesting trip.

Besides driving a standard car, we were also driving in a car that had no air conditioning. Three months earlier after a good tax rebate, I was in the market for a new-to-me car – simply put, a car that wasn't new but was 'new-to-me'.

My grandmother brought me to Montague, after some of my classes in Charlottetown at the University of Prince Edward Island. I saw the add on the internet for the standard car that was only four-years-old, low kilometers, and all for a ridiculously low price but, it had no options.

The guy I was buying the car from wasn't at home. He would be there in about a half hour, but my grandmother couldn't wait. She had plans and the weather was already compromising her time. I wanted the car, so I stayed behind.

"Well," I said when the guy finally came, "I guess I'm going to buy it." And that's the story of how I bought a used car without even going for a test drive.

The car was a great buy. It had a Bluetooth radio, but it had roll windows and no air conditioning. When you buy a car in the winter, you forget how much you'll actually miss air conditioning in the dead heat of summer.

∞

It just happened that the weekend we were going to Halifax was probably one of the hottest weekends of the summer. It was the type of day that the sun was scorching hot and drained one's energy. Arms got sunburned just sitting in a car. Clothes would cling to skin and foreheads were damp with sweat.

The Queen Victoria General Hospital is located downtown in Halifax, not a fun first-time drive in the city. Traffic in Halifax was different from Tignish. The busiest that traffic ever got in Tignish was after church or on a bingo night.

The hotel we had booked was probably one of the fanciest hotels we had ever stayed at. Usually, when we stayed at hotels, cheap was best. This hotel was near the hospital, only a short few mile walk.

As fancy as the hotel was, the hospital was the opposite. The hospital was old and dirty. Never had I seen such horrible conditions for a place where people were supposed to heal. If people hadn't been inside, I would have believed it was abandoned. The elevator doors opened on every single floor without provocation. One elevator seemed to be broken for the entire time that Dad was there, which if I remember correctly was near eleven weeks. The faucet in the public bathroom was just not there. The water in the entire building wasn't safe to consume. It had legionnaire's disease and there was no promise it would ever be fixed. Some of the windows were broken and covered with boards. There was no working air conditioning. There were only massive fans in the hallways which seemed to provide a warm air at best.

On Sunday morning of that weekend, we had to leave to go home. The problem with leaving was that I parked in an underground park and the ticket booth was halfway up the hill. This doesn't sound like it would be an issue but if you ever drove a standard; you know stopping halfway up the hill is difficult when there is a car close behind.

"What do I do?" I asked Mom. "If I dare to take my foot off the brakes, I may go backward and hit him."

Mom hesitated, "I'll go and ask him to back up a little. Tell him we need a little room."

She didn't have the chance to get out of the car before the guy caught on and he backed up. The next hurdle was that I was driving to a busy street and because it was a hill, it was a give it all scenario. With a quick prayer, I pressed my foot on the gas pedal and hoped nothing came as I stopped to turn in the middle of the street.

The room Dad was in was tiny. There were six beds in the room and it was hard to fit a chair inside the curtains. It was obvious how uncomfortable Dad was in the room. On the island, most of the wards only had four beds and they were not co-ed.

One of the major disadvantages of the ward was that there was a clear lack of privacy. We could hear all the conversations between the doctors, nurses, and the other patients. It was difficult, especially if they were getting bad news.

∞

One patient, I remember vividly was an elderly woman who was not completely fluent in the English language. She had a loving husband and a supporting family. Her health was declining and the hospital was pushing for her to be moved to a long-term facility, but her family was just not prepared. It was very sad.

In the midst of the many consultations with social workers and doctors, she was left alone. She got up to get herself something to drink.

As she was about to turn on the faucet, Dad looked at her carefully, "You can't drink the water. It'll make you sick."

She nodded her head and smiled. Apparently, the lack of understanding of the English language left her unable to understand what he was saying and she quickly poured herself a drink. By the time that the nurses arrived after Dad had pressed the buzzer, she had downed two glasses. Legionnaire's Disease is a type of pneumonia caused by Legionella bacteria and it is contracted from water filled with the bacteria. She was definitely exposed.

∞

I stayed at one of the city's university's summer residence that night. I walked from the hospital. I left my car in the hospital parking lot, despite the many protests from Dad.

Halifax isn't the safest city. We've all heard the stories - it's overcrowded with a high presence of gang activity. Well, I am the first to say I am naïve. I didn't want the hassle of driving my standard car through the city. So, I walked downtown Halifax with a large kit bag attached to my neck, completely lost when it was dark outside. I must have had an angel protecting me because I later heard on the radio about an attack that took place on that same street, and around those streets, the same night.

The next day, when I was getting ready to leave Halifax to go home, I couldn't help but be a little frightened about the possible parking fees. They charged a lot of money to park because they wanted to discourage staff from using the parking lot.

Before I left the hospital, I went to the washroom. Before my brother joined the military, he worked security at the hospital in Charlottetown. He explained that if someone looked like they were very upset, they usually let them leave for free. I thought I would give it a chance.

I splashed water in my eyes and walked to my car. I thought of my saddest memory and tried to look the saddest that I could ever look. I drove to the booth prepared to give my Emmy worthy performance. The guy in the booth was listening loudly to the most upbeat music I have ever heard. His body was moving along to the beat of the music. Still, I tried to look sad. Two days and an overnight of parking probably racked up to near $50 of charges. I'm not sure if he even noticed the tears in my eyes or if he just didn't care.

"That'll be $27," the attendant said plainly.

I passed him my money, pleased it wasn't more. My Emmy-worthy performance wasn't so Emmy-worthy after all.

The next time that Mom and I went to visit Dad in Halifax, we stayed at Dalhousie's summer residence instead of the Lord Nelson Hotel & Suites. Dalhousie was financially a better place to stay but lacked the luxury. Instead of walking like I had done by myself, I bravely drove down the busy streets.

Not sure of where the proper place to park was, I parked at the university's parking lot that may have even been further away from the hospital. At least the walking was mostly on the campus.

By the time we got our room key, we were exhausted. The thought of our room being on the third floor was almost depressing.

"Just a few more minutes and we will be in our room," Mom encouraged, her eyes shimmering with glee.

We huffed and we puffed as we entered the second floor.

"Can we give ourselves a break?" she asked, exhausted.

I nodded in agreement.

"Look Atara," she pointed to an elevator, looking relieved.

"I don't know if we should use it," I said, looking around for signs.

"It wouldn't be here if we couldn't use it," she argued.

So, we walked over to the elevator.

"Okay," I said, pressing the button. As I pressed the button. Alarms started to ring.

"Let's get out of here," Mom suggested as if we were common criminals.

In our attempt to flee we found another set of stairs. These steps were even narrower than the previous set we were on. It was almost like our penance for being lazy.

∞

One of the procedures they had done for Dad in Halifax was a new feeding tube. It completely bypassed his stomach and was inserted into the intestine. The feeding tube also had a drainage output that caught the stomach fluids. It was essentially a bag attached to his tube inserted into his stomach. The stuff that drained from his stomach was disgusting - the smelliest and brownest contents you could ever imagine. On the upside, it saved him from getting sick as often as he did in the past. It also helped a lot with his nausea. It didn't completely stop the nausea or the vomiting, but it helped.

A few more weeks later, Mom had done a separate trip alone and then we had done one more trip together. Dad was transferred back to Prince County Hospital in Summerside. Unlike the previous times when Dad was in Prince County Hospital and we minded the drive, it now didn't seem so bad.

∞

It didn't take long before he was sent back to Western Hospital in Alberton. He was doing quite well and we were starting to have hope he was coming home soon.

The plan was for Dad to regain his strength and come home. The problem with our plan was that we had no coverage for his feeding tube formula or his medications. With his fist fills of pills and the specialty formula for his feeding tube the cost was more than what we could afford.

Some of the programs that were in place to help weren't applicable to us. I still lived at home and my salary, combined with my parents, made our income too high. It didn't matter that I didn't have guaranteed work or I brought Dad to his appointments because Mom was working. We went to politicians and to anyone else who would listen to our story.

As we struggled to find a way to pay for Dad's medication and to bring him home, Amy was also finding herself in a difficult position.

She was struggling with the pressures of single parenting because Landon was on tour. Hallie and Ben both demanded a lot of her attention and energy and she was exhausted.

Sometimes Mom and I would take Ben to give Amy a much-needed break. He was comfortable enough with us that he could stay for several days at a time. He didn't even mind when we brought him to the hospital to visit Dad.

In late November, Landon came home from his tour. Because it was a day off from work for me, I would make the trip to Halifax to pick Landon up. Ben was coming with me. Landon really wanted to see him.

I took a deep breath, silently praying that he would change his mind. I was going to have a four-year-old and Dad in the car, and I knew Dad would add to the work. How was he going to sit in a car for over eight hours when he spent most of his days laying in a bed? There was nothing I could say. I wouldn't dare hurt his feelings and ask him not to go. He wanted to go.

The next morning, after a night shift, I picked Ben up from my aunt's house. Mom had dropped him off before she went to work.

"Do you know what we are going to do today?" I asked Ben excitedly.

He shook his head, "No."

"We're going to pick up your Daddy!" I told him.

Ben sighed and didn't say anything.

Thinking he didn't really hear me, I repeated again, "We are going to get your Daddy at the airport."

He looked at me in disbelief as if I had just said the craziest thing that he had ever heard, "Don't say that, Auntie A."

"Why not?" I asked, intrigued. "Don't you want to go and get him?"

"I can't believe it," he says, covering his eyes in disgust, "and I won't believe it."

"You'll see that Daddy is really coming home today," I promised, as I lifted him in his car seat.

We went to pick up Dad at Western Hospital. He kept telling the nurses that he was going to Halifax, but I don't think that they believed him until I got there.

Ben kept insisting that he wanted to push Grampy's wheelchair out, although he could not see over the chair and he had a strong desire to push the chair towards the wall. Both Dad and I allowed him to assert his independence.

∞

"I'll drive first," Dad eagerly suggested.

"Dad," I said looking at him with a small sigh, "I'm not really sure if you should be driving."

Mom had lectured me several times the day before that it would be best if Dad didn't drive. She didn't want him to get tired.

"Why?" he asked, the irritated tone in his voice evident.

"Because you haven't driven for a while now," I replied, trying to choose my words carefully.

"Take me back inside," he replied.

"Okay, okay," I blurted, wanting to avoid hurting Dad's feelings. "You can drive until we get to the bridge."

The bridge separating Prince Edward Island and New Brunswick was an hour and a half away. Traffic wouldn't be that busy on a weekday and it seemed like a fair compromise.

"We will see," he replied as he slid into the driver's seat.

In the four hours that it took to get to the airport, Dad finally let me drive. Ben watched a movie, ate two snacks, and fell asleep. No matter how hard I tried to convince Ben otherwise, he still did not believe I was taking him to get his father.

"I'll go and find Landon," I commanded after I parked in the airport parking lot. "His flight should be in soon."

"You can't," Dad said, pointing to Ben who was still napping in the backseat. "He has grown attached to you. If he wakes up and it's only me here, he will be pretty upset. I'll go."

"I'll wake him up and we can all go in together," I suggested, not wanting Dad to go in by himself. It was a long walk and he hadn't walked any amount of distances in a long time.

Gently, I nudged Ben until he woke up.

"We have to go inside now."

"I don't want to walk," he said. "Carry me, Auntie A."

For at least a two kilometer walk, I carried Ben, who no longer felt so light. I prayed that Dad wouldn't lose his strength and gave him options to sit near the entrance where there were chairs.

"I'm fine," he responded.

I offered to find a wheelchair, which he refused.

"I can walk," he promised.

After we found where we were supposed to be, we sat and waited. Landon still hadn't come through the doors yet.

Ben still looked confused as to why we were there. He sat quietly. His eyes roaming around the room. Then the doors opened. Young, old, different ethnicities of people came through, but Landon still hadn't. Near the end, Landon finally came through the doors!

∞

"It's Daddy!" Ben exclaimed. "Can I go to him, Auntie A?"

I nodded. Ben ran to his father and wrapped his little arms around his legs, "I missed you, Daddy."

Landon lifted him in his arms, "I missed you, Ben."

Finally, Landon looked at Dad. A few months had passed since Landon had seen Dad.

"I can't believe that you're here."

A few months later Landon shared that when he left for his tour, he thought he would come home early for a funeral - Dad's funeral. What a bittersweet feeling for Dad to be well enough to greet him at the airport and to push Landon's luggage cart out to the car.

The C Word

"Once you choose hope, anything's possible."
Christopher Reeve

The c word, that awful c word. We've all heard it before. Yet every time we hear it, it's enough to make the little hairs stand straight up on the back of our necks. With good reason, that six letter word may be just one of the most feared word in the English language. It's probably safe to say that we've all been affected by this horrible disease. It does not discriminate: young, old, male, female, rich and poor - cancer knows no boundaries.

My paternal grandfather was diagnosed in his early sixties with colon cancer that had spread. I was about six-years-old when he got sick. His prognosis was not good as he was only given six months to live when he was first diagnosed. He was supposed to retire soon and enjoy the rest of his life. It was going to be his time to relax after all of his hard years of working. The diagnosis didn't seem fair. He lasted 18 months, one year longer than what the doctors expected. Dad was devastated when Papa passed away.

Papa was Dad's hero even if they weren't always the closest. Papa was a sports fanatic and Dad, unlike his brother, was not very good at sports. He tried hockey but his feet were flat and skates hurt them. When Dad started to work, they would sometimes have disagreements about the way they should fix some of the machinery at the business. Really, the arguments really boiled down to be a bit more significant about who the better mechanic was. Dad felt that Papa offered better wages and benefits to some of the other workers than he did to Dad. Papa probably never saw Dad as the adult he had become and instead seen him as a child.

At the end of the day, despite their differences, they loved each other. One of the last conversations that Mom had with Papa was about Dad. Summer was just about to begin, and Papa was worried that Dad was doing too much with Landon and me.

"Please don't let Trevor go to the beach on those hot days, Lorna," Papa begged. "That sun is too strong and it's too hard for him to chase the kids around."

I was eight when Papa died, but I can still remember his death. He was buried on the hill in the cemetery overlooking the family farm in Truro, Nova Scotia. It was his request. It was early in July and the weather allowed for a beautiful day. It certainly wasn't a day you wanted to spend saying goodbye to someone you loved so much.

After the service was over, Dad climbed the hilly terrain at the edge of the cemetery. Everyone but my grandmother, aunts, uncle, my mother, and Landon and I had left by that point.

I remember how Dad stood quietly and gazed at the fields and the tears started to fall from his eyes.

"This shouldn't have happened," he sobbed. "I should have gone before him."

Dad never really got over the loss of Papa. As time passed, it got easier to deal with. He learned new ways to live without Papa. And as the months and years went by, we talked less and less about the times when Papa was sick and talked more about the happier memories.

∞

Colon cancer can be hereditary. Which is why, every so often, Dad would have a colonoscopy. One of the last times that Dad went to have one was before Ben was born. They found polyps. Polyps are fairly common growths in the colon. Luckily, Dad's polyps were benign. As a precaution, Dad was told that he should have colonoscopies more frequently.

In December of 2015, Dad was scheduled to have a colonoscopy. Apparently, when he was a patient at the Victoria General, something was found. It wasn't on the priority list to fix at that time. They had bigger fish to fry. They wanted him to gain weight and strength before they even looked into it.

The first time they tried to do a colonoscopy in December, it didn't go over great. Well actually, it was more like a nightmare. He kept getting sick from the medications that were supposed to clean his system and because his feedings had to stop, his blood sugars kept going low. Even if it wasn't done right, they knew he definitely had polyps. They needed to do the test again in the New Year which meant we had to go through the holidays wondering if he had cancer or not.

"Can I go home today for Christmas?" Dad asked on the 23rd of December. He was still a patient at Western Hospital in Alberton.

Besides, another weekend in early December, Christmas was the first time Dad was going home since February. The original plan to have him discharged by Christmas would not be possible, but we were grateful to get him home, even if it was just for a little bit. He was really looking forward to spending a night or two in his own bed.

A few hours later, with a few pages of instructions from the nurses and a box of supplies, we were on our way home for Christmas. I had not seen Dad that excited in a while. It made me realize how lucky I was. A little thing, like spending a few days in his own home, meant the world to Dad. Dad didn't have it the worst, not by a long shot. He was lucky to be born in Canada where he was privileged with health care. He had a family who loved him, but he really didn't have the freedom to stay in his own house for long.

Landon, Amy, and the kids were staying at Nena's house since she had already left to spend the winter in Ontario at my aunts' houses. They wanted us to spend Christmas at Nena's house with them and we agreed.

∞

We arrived at Nena's house just after lunch. It was going to be an exciting Christmas. It was Hallie's first Christmas, and Ben was starting to understand that Santa was coming to bring him presents. Dad was going to be spending Christmas in his childhood home and we would all be together for Christmas.

We made our Christmas lobster chowder. Lobster chowder on Christmas Eve was our family tradition for as long as I could remember. We waited for Santa to pass by Nena's house on the fire truck, just like he had when Landon and I were young. Before the kids went to bed, they listened to the classic *The Night Before Christmas,* but this time it was Landon's turn to read the story.

While Amy was settling the kids for sleep, Dad checked his blood sugars and we were surprised that they were low, 3.7. Now, 3.7 is not a dangerously low blood sugar, but for Dad, it might as well have been. Dad's blood sugars were unstable most of the time. They dropped quickly and he didn't feel the effects and we couldn't see any symptoms of a low blood sugar. It was often hard to get his blood sugars to rise because he would get sick immediately after drinking or eating.

The good part was that if you were going to have a low blood sugar level, Christmas seemed the best time. We gave Dad fudge, candies, cookies, and anything else that we could find that might stay down long enough to raise his blood sugars.

"Let's check them again," Mom commanded like an army sergeant.

Dad nodded and washed his hands with a washcloth. It happened in the past that his blood sugars raised to a 7 after he had something to raise them. We thought we were home-free, but it turned out he had sugar on his hands from the food we were feeding him. I never made that mistake again.

"2.8," I replied, checking it once more.

"They're getting lower," Mom said with a disappointed sigh.

"Just give it a chance," Dad said, "It's only been twenty minutes."

"No," she replied. The panic was evident in her tone. "We need to get them a little higher right now. We need to find you something else to eat."

"I can't eat anymore right now," he replied.

"Then pick something to drink," she responded.

"I'll have a glass of pop," he said after mulling it over.

Landon got up quickly and went to the fridge, "We only have diet pop."

"Put sugar in it," I suggested.

Landon added a few tablespoons of sugar in the glass of pop.

"Drink it all," Mom ordered.

Dad did as he was asked. With a frown on his face, he gulped down the pop.

"I've got to go to the bathroom," he said as he placed the glass in the sink.

Once he got inside the bathroom, we heard the door click.

"He just locked the door," I remarked.

"Trevor!" Mom said panicked, "open the door right now."

"No," Dad replied bluntly. "I'm using the bathroom."

"Dad, you need to open the door!" Landon said, firmly. He looked at Mom and I. "Should I break it open?"

"I'll open the door when I'm done. Don't you dare break it," he responded with anger.

We waited until we heard the toilet flush.

"Open the door now!" We all said.

"I have to wash my hands!" he said, staunchly.

Isn't it the times that you want someone to rush that they take longer than usual? After what seemed like ages, he finally opened the door.

"Let's check your blood sugars," Mom said.

"Not yet," he responded.

"Maybe he should go back to the hospital," Landon suggested.

Mom glanced at Dad to see his reaction. Taking him back to the hospital was the last thing she wanted. If we couldn't handle an episode of low blood sugar, how could Dad ever come home?

"No," Dad said firmly. "I'll be fine."

"Then have a drink," Mom stated.

"No," he stated, "I'm not drinking pop with sugar. It's gross!"

"The kids have chocolate milk. Do you want some of that instead?" Landon asked.

Dad nodded, "I'll have some chocolate milk."

I tried to sign to Landon to add some sugar into the chocolate milk to make it even sweeter, but Landon was not catching on. Dad did.

"You can put some sugar in it," Dad agreed, "but don't add any more than two tablespoons."

Once again, Dad gulped down the drink.

"Can we check your blood sugars now?" I asked.

"Okay," he stated.

After a quick wash of his hands, a dab of his finger with the needle, and allowing the blood to seep on the chem strip, it gave us his new blood sugar reading.

"5.1," I shared.

"That's still a little low," Mom said.

"It's not bad," Dad remarked.

By this time, it was three in the morning. I had to work the day shift the next day, and we were all tired.

"Let's go to bed. I'll set my alarm and check them again soon."

By the time morning had come, Dad's blood sugars had reached 20.6 with the help of his tube feeds. It was a learning experience for us because at the hospital Dad was constantly hooked to his tube feedings. For most of the previous day and evening, he had not been hooked to a machine. We learned that his insulin dosage needed to be frequently adjusted. Learning to have Dad at home without a team of health care professionals, was certainly a learning experience for all of us.

∞

I took him to his next colonoscopy in January. I hated driving with Dad when he was in pain. He felt every bump in the road. He wouldn't usually say anything, but he would moan and I knew he felt it.

Panic set in for me when no one called me from the hospital, once Dad's procedure was supposed to be finished. My first thought was that he must be full of cancer. I tried to think of other possibilities that would cause them to take longer than what they expected. A low blood sugar, difficulty finding a vein, a long time going through the history - but my mind kept thinking cancer, I wasn't sure why.

When I got to the hospital, I rushed to the recovery section where Dad was so I could try to catch what the doctor was telling him. The doctor was everything that you would imagine in a young surgeon: precise and extremely competent. He was exactly the doctor you wanted working on your loved one.

∞

Despite Dad's many health concerns, it wasn't this doctor's first rodeo. The doctor was well-trained; in fact, some of his training was by the gastroenterologist that he had seen in Halifax. This doctor was completely prepared for the challenges that Dad presented.

He told us we had to book an office visit. It made little sense for him to discuss any findings with Dad when Dad was still feeling the effects of the sedation from the colonoscopy.

I called his office the next day for an appointment. On Friday, I signed Dad out of the hospital for a weekend pass, and we went to Charlottetown that afternoon for his office visit to discuss the findings of the colonoscopy.

They were calling for bad weather that evening, and we wondered if we should even go, but we wanted to know what was going on. I always wanted to be aware, even if it was bad news. If I knew, I figured at least I could try to come up with a game plan. I could feel like I had power in the situation. If I didn't know, all I could do was imagine the millions of different scenarios that could play out - usually, none of them ended well in my mind.

Dad had polyps. He was going to need surgery to get the polyps out. The polyps would then be biopsied, and we would know if he was going to need any chemotherapy or radiation. I nodded my head, politely. Years of experience led me to the conclusion that no medical appointment with Dad was ever quick.

It wasn't easy to give Dad's medical history. It may have been easier to answer what health problems Dad didn't have, instead of what he did have. It was also hard to explain it all. It was a bit overwhelming to be sure that all the needed details were given and nothing was missed. I wasn't old enough, growing up when my father was sick, where I could really remember word-for-word accounts of what went wrong with his health or what he had done. There was so much wrong with his health and so many procedures that he had. Some of the details of my father's health seemed like they couldn't possibly be true. Dad couldn't usually remember all the fine details. He usually looked at me like I was supposed to know it all.

"I'd like to use local anesthesia, which means that you would be awake for the surgery," the doctor stated.

"No," Dad replied, stunned, "I really don't want to be awake."

"I'm concerned about the strain on your neck because you've had a fracture," he replied. "We would have to turn your body when you would be unconscious."

Dad's expression instantly changed. He was horrified.

The doctor sighed.

"If you are really against being awake, we could do a small part of the surgery where you would be awake and do the majority of the surgery when you would be under anesthesia."

Dad nodded at the compromise, "I can live with that."

"On the day of your surgery, be sure to take your morning blood sugars and your full dose of insulin even though you can't eat," the doctor advised Dad.

"You don't want to do that with him," I warned. "We are about two hours away from Charlottetown, and his blood sugars drop quickly. Can we decrease the amount of insulin?"

He hummed. He looked at some of the information inside of Dad's chart.

"Maybe we can arrange for you to be admitted here the night before the surgery. That way you won't have to worry about it."

"Okay," Dad said, "are you sure that you can't change the schedule so that you would be working that day?"

The doctor laughed.

"No, but I can promise that you'll be in good hands."

∞

By the time that we got back to Western Hospital, the staff at the Queen Elizabeth Hospital had already called. They had decided that they were going to admit him at Queen Elizabeth to get him prepped for surgery. He needed another blood transfusion, and his potassium level was low. They would call soon when they had a bed that was available for him.

"Do you know if they will have a bed soon?" I asked one of the nurses as she came in the room to give Dad some medication that evening.

"No," the nurse said, "we won't know until they call us back."

By this time, Mom had arrived. We filled her in on what was going on. As Dad and I, she was a little confused as to why Dad was going to be admitted to Queen Elizabeth Hospital when Western Hospital was an acute hospital. Regardless of the reasoning, we wanted the best care for Dad, and if it meant going to Charlottetown, he would be there.

A few hours had passed, and still, we had not heard back from Queen Elizabeth Hospital. It was starting to play on our nerves because the evening was starting to pass and arrangements would have to be made if he had to go the following day.

"He can't be going tonight?" Mom asked the nurse. Although it was a question, it came out as more of a statement.

The nurse glanced at the clock.

"No, probably not. I'll give them a call and see what they say."

"I've got to go to work tomorrow," I stated after the nurse left the room. "How is he going to get back down?"

"We will figure it out," Mom replied. "We will try to find someone in the family that could take him down."

The nurse came back in, "They'll call in the morning, but they want him down there before 9:00 AM."

"I have family sick time," I explained to Mom and Dad. "I'll find someone to work for four hours. It'll give me enough time to get you down there before 9:00 AM and be back to work by noon."

"Are you sure that you can do that?" Mom asked.

"Yeah," I said, looking through my contacts on my phone to find someone to replace me.

∞

The next morning, I arrived at the hospital bright and early, prepared to make the quick trip with Dad to Charlottetown and get back to work. Unfortunately, the universe was working against us.

"They haven't called yet," Dad said, irritated.

"Don't panic," I said. "We still have a little bit of time left."

The next half hour had come and gone. The clock still ticked away. An hour soon passed, and we were still waiting. At this point, I would not have enough time to go and get back in time for work.

"They aren't ready for him yet," I said after I had called Mom, "and I am running out of time."

"Okay," she said, taking a deep breath, "this is what we are going to do. I'm going to give my niece a quick call and see if there is any way that she could take him down."

Mom's niece worked seasonally. She was also probably the most selfless person that I have ever met. If she could help us out, she would.

"Let me know how you get along," I said.

As it turned out, she was able to help us out and drive Dad.

∞

Traveling with Dad almost required a training manual. Blood sugars needed to be checked, bumps in the road needed to be avoided, and corners had to be taken lightly. Still, sometimes that wasn't enough.

Before they left Alberton, Dad warned her as he got in her brand-new car, "You might have to stop in a hurry because I could get sick."

Dad's surgery, which ended up to be scheduled at the beginning of the following week, was the same day as my final exam that was scheduled a month in advance. It was also my first day off. I was just getting off from a night shift that morning.

We expected that Dad would be brought to the pre-surgery area by the time we got there. We were glad to avoid one pre-surgery "if anything should happen to me" speech although Mom had heard the majority of the spiel on the phone that morning.

It seemed like we had to let him say his piece. He needed to get it off his chest because surgery was still surgery. There was always that chance that something could go wrong but the talk stopped being effective many surgeries ago. In my mind, Dad was going to outlive our whole family so a "just in case" talk was kind of a moot point.

The surgery was supposed to be three hours, the same time it would take for me to write my final exam. There was a good chance that I would be back at the hospital by the time they brought him to recovery.

My final took less time than expected, two hours, and Dad had only been taken to OR for about an hour and a half by the time I had arrived. I had only been waiting with them for a few minutes when Dad was being wheeled by.

Immediately, I had flashbacks of the story of my great-grandmother that was told to me on numerous occasions over the years. It was in the twenties when medicine was not as advanced as it is now. My great-grandfather put her on a train to go to the states to be seen by doctors. She was having a lot of pain in her stomach so they opened her up to do an exploratory surgery and then they closed her up quickly. She was full of cancer. It was everywhere. Was the same thing, decades later, happening to my father? It made me queasy just thinking about it.

Once Dad was back in his room, Dad wiped the tears away from his eyes. We still did not understand what was going on, but it was not good. I glanced at Mom who looked as if she had aged ten years in a matter of minutes. I struggled to find my next breath.

"Has the doctor talked to you yet?" One of the nurses asked Mom and me.

"No," Mom replied solemnly, "we haven't spoken to anyone yet."

"Well, they couldn't go ahead with the surgery. They could not get a line in. The plan is to go back in, in a few days, and they will try again."

"Thank you for letting us know what is going on," Mom said as the nurses were leaving the room.

"Are you okay, Dad?" I asked.

"I just wanted them to do the surgery today," Taking a deep breath, he continued, "I want to go home."

"I know," I said, just as discouraged. "They will do the surgery and you will come home soon."

∞

The surgery was exactly two weeks later. They were prepared for Dad's challenges this time. Earlier that week they had put in three access lines. What stopped them on their first attempt at surgery surely wouldn't stop them again.

Mom and I waited in the little waiting room while he was gone to the OR. Her nerves were getting the best of her and they were starting to get the best of me. We watched the door, from the time he went in until he was being wheeled by. We were both on edge - our ears focused on anything being moved by on wheels. We feared that something was going to go wrong or they wouldn't be able to do the surgery.

Two and a half hours later, Dad was being taken back to his room. The surgery had progressed and been completed. He was just coming out of the anesthesia, and he looked tired. My eyes narrowed in on Mom's eyes.

"Should we be worried? It didn't take as long as they expected."

"I'm not sure," she answered honestly, "but all that matters right now is that he got through surgery."

We followed the porters. This time they brought him to the ICU. We knew after surgery, he would go there. He had a lot of health history and pain management would be better dealt with in ICU.

"Wait here," one porter said, pointing to a new waiting room. "They'll want to get him settled and the doctor usually stops here to let you know how he got along."

Waiting was becoming habitual. Mom and I were getting good at it. Within some time, I'm not sure how much time, the doctor came in the waiting room.

"He got along great, better than what we could have expected. We did everything we needed to do."

"Thank God," Mom replied.

For the first time all day, my shoulders relaxed and my heart rate slowed. I could finally relax. We visited Dad for a few minutes, but I still had to work a night shift. I had only taken three hours off and was expected to be at work by 9:00 PM.

When Mom and I went out to the car, I tried to start the car. It wouldn't start. The battery was completely drained.

"I think it's the bolt on the battery," I told Mom. "It needs to be tightened."

A few weeks before, like the previous summer, the radio had refused to shut off when I turned the car off. I unscrewed the bolts on the battery to manually force the radio to shut off, but I probably didn't tighten them enough and they had become loose causing the battery to die. I grabbed the wrench in the truck, popped open the engine bonnet, and went to work trying to tighten the bolts. With any luck, once it had power, the car would start easily. I was happy to know a bit about cars. Some people don't know how to pump their own gas. Our roadside assistance had run out about a month earlier and the company's prices had increased drastically. Finding a new package was yet another thing that was still on our to-do list. I was really hoping to avoid calling a tow truck.

Well, the wrench was smaller in size than what I should have used and it got stuck between the positive and negative sides of the battery. It was smoking and a small flame quickly started. I started to blow on the flame but the fire, although still small, was quickly getting larger. Blowing on the fire was not having any effect. For what I felt I did know about cars, I did not know what to do next.

"You need to do more than blow a small puff of air," Mom said as she quickly took another wrench from the car. She hit the wrench that was stuck until it eventually fell. We were lucky because I imagine it could have gotten much worse. Some nice men in the parking lot noticed we were having car troubles. They came over to help us before we managed to burn the entire hospital down. The fire went out.

"Let's jump start it," one of them suggested.

The car quickly started. We were set to go home, as long as I didn't stall, which was an obstacle to get past all on its own.

"I think you're going to need a new starter," another man told us.

"Thanks for the help. I will bring it to our mechanic to see if he can fix it. My father just had surgery and this is the last thing I needed right now." I explained, allowing them to believe I was clueless. It was too long of a story to explain anything else.

"I know the feeling," one of the men said. "My wife has been in the hospital for the past month."

I wanted to tell him that Dad's been in the hospital for the majority of the last two years, but I thought better of it. We thanked them and set out. On the way home, the sun was setting. It was getting dark out.

∞

"Do you have your lights on?" Mom asked.

"They should be," I replied, but as we drove to a part of the road where there were no street lights, I doubted we had any lights.

I pulled over, "You have to check Mom. I'm too scared to take my foot off the clutch. I might stall."

She quickly got out and checked. When she got back to the car, she stated, "They aren't working."

I flicked the lights and they came back on.

"They're working now," I responded.

A few minutes later, the lights stopped working again. I flicked them, this time twice before they worked again. The lights flicked off and on most of the way home. We drove slowly and I pulled over every time I could see the lights of another car. We hoped that a friend of ours who lived in Wellington was home but our prayers went unanswered because her house was in darkness.

"I'll keep driving," I told Mom. "You pray that the lights stay on."

Mom called Nena. We would leave our car at the O'Leary corner and take Nena's car home. We were about twenty minutes from O'Leary when the car died. I started to cry. I was running out of time before I had to get to work. I feared how much it would cost to have the car towed and the repairs. I was stressed.

"Stop crying," Mom tried to console me. "Let's just get the tow truck."

"Can our winter get any worse?" I asked, referring to everything that had gone on in the past few weeks.

"Yeah, it can," she answered. "We could have lost your father today!"

I stayed quiet. She was right.

The tow truck came and towed the car to the mechanics. He gave us a drive home and I drove Mom's car to work. We didn't dare tell Dad about our journey home. He would have told us we were too rough on the car.

∞

Dad spent several days, probably close to a week, in ICU before being moved to the floor. After another week or so, he was transferred back to Western Hospital, and Dad excelled in his recovery.

Things were starting to work out. He was able to come home. Dad really appreciated being home. He was grateful to be in his own house.

∞

In April, Dad had a consultation with the surgeon who had taken the polyps out. Since the surgery, Dad's strength to walk long distances had improved. He wasn't as pale as he was before. Even the doctor had noticed the changes in Dad.

"I am confident I got it all out," the doctor explained, "but it was cancer so I should send you to an oncologist. The oncologist will decide if you need any chemotherapy or radiation, but I don't think you will."

Several weeks later, Dad and I found ourselves once again traveling to Charlottetown for the appointment. Although I drove, there was once again a huge difference in Dad. He was getting stronger. His mood had lightened and he was the father I had always known him to be. He wasn't as fragile as before. Being home was making all the difference in the world and things were starting to go back to normal.

Once again, we talked to the nurses and the doctor explaining, to the best of our abilities as well as we could, about Dad's health. Perhaps it was a help that he had a thick chart from his many trips and admissions to the hospital – it was almost like our words weren't needed at all.

"With the way that your stomach is, I don't believe chemotherapy is even an option," the oncologist explained. "We could do radiation but I don't think we will."

"You can," I quickly replied. My fear was they were avoiding treatment because of Dad's past medical history. He was strong and if radiation was what was best, then I wanted him to have the radiation. Dad was a fighter.

"We'll keep a close eye on everything, but right now it's not needed," he explained.

∞

That summer, they had done another colonoscopy to be sure that there were no other polyps.

Like all the other colonoscopies, the biggest challenge was his blood sugars. The milk feedings had to be stopped supposedly three days before the colonoscopy but it was unrealistic. His blood sugars kept dropping. Stopping his tube feedings one day before the colonoscopy was all he could handle.

Since Dad had come home with his latest feeding tube, I had done many searches on the internet about feeding tubes. I didn't know many people who had feeding tubes and I wanted to learn more.

One of my biggest fears was someone would suggest that Dad should be transferred to a manor. He was in his early fifties and should have been dealing with a mid-life crisis. I didn't want him sent to a place to live out the remaining days of his life. Mom and I both wanted Dad at home and we were willing to do the work to make it possible.

Every night we searched the internet, trying to learn a little more each day. One tip constantly mentioned was using pop to unclog the tube. If the harsh acid of pop could be inserted into a tube, then we were willing to stop making Dad drink energy drinks and insert the drinks into his tube to treat a low blood sugar.

The day of the colonoscopy had come. Once again, my schedule was open to take Dad down to his appointment. I sat with him this time for a great deal longer than the previous time. They allowed me to go so far with him before they told me I could come back.

This time I was called earlier than expected. They hadn't been able to get a line again. Dad was given the choice of coming back, probably being admitted beforehand, or doing the procedure without sedation. He chose to do it without sedation. He wasn't staying in the hospital unless he really needed to. No polyps were found and I thanked God. His next colonoscopy was due in a year's time.

On the way home, Dad was in a lot of pain but yet he stated, "With all of those polyps they found before, I'm not sure why they couldn't do that test every six months."

I chuckled.

"I'm sure you're their favorite patient to do colonoscopies on. You can't get the medication down. Your blood sugars keep dropping, and they can't get an IV line. If they had their way, they'd probably never do another colonoscopy on you again."

He took a minute to think about what I said and then mumbled, just loud enough for me to hear, "I guess it was another time I got lucky."

Saying Goodbye

"Someday when the pages of my life end, I know that you will be one of its most beautiful chapters."

Unknown

If you were to take the time to search the internet for hints about how to write a book, you would be surprised by the millions of tips that come up. Some of the tips are helpful and useful. Some of the tips are not so helpful. A few of the tips, like writing a novel after you've consumed a point of alcohol, seem crazy. By the sound of that tip, the effects of alcohol work in different ways for some people than it does for me.

One author suggested starting at the beginning and then write the conclusion before the middle of the novel. The theory behind it is to encourage the writer to fill in the gaps when the dreaded writer's block hits. I thought this might be a way to ensure that I complete at least one book in my lifetime.

The problem was I wasn't sure how I wanted to write my ending. My life isn't over so how can I complete writing the chapters of the rest of my life? How did I want the readers to feel when they were finished reading what I had written? Should it be happy and inspiring? I'm a huge soap opera fan. Would it be fair to end with a huge cliff-hanger? Maybe some of the readers would beg me to have mercy and write a sequel.

After much thought, inspiration, and a few curse words every now and then, I can now tell you it will not end in a cliff-hanger. Instead, it ends at the end of an era and the hardest thing I ever had to do: saying goodbye.

∞

Most of us must say goodbye to our parents at one point or another in our life. It's the natural order. Some of us face this loss at a young age while others are luckier. Some must grieve the loss as a time of missed opportunities with a parent they really didn't know well.

Movies and books try to expose us to what grief may feel like. We witness our friends, family, and neighbors impacted by a loss but until it happens to you or I, it is hard to describe the pain. Grief is a subjective pain. It's difficult to describe and different for everyone. Just as unique and special as our relationships with our parents are, so is the pain of losing them.

∞

Months have passed since Dad has passed away and there aren't many hours in the day that my mind doesn't think about him. I play videos with his voice, trying to wrap my brain around the idea that the recordings are the only time I will ever hear his voice again. I look at photos stored on my phone, computer, or protected in photo albums. I begged Landon to send me all the photos he has of Dad. I try to remember our conversations and all the advice he had given me throughout the years. I don't even remember the last thing he told me.

Mom and I have had debates many times as to whether or not Dad knew he was dying. I've analyzed all the conversations I remember, searching for clues. I refuse to believe he wouldn't have told us if he knew. Dad loved life so much. He would have been devastated to know he was dying. He wouldn't have been able to keep it a secret.

Instead, the months before he passed away, Dad and I talked about Christmas. We planned our perfect Christmas. We even shopped on the internet for gifts for Mom. We talked about work. He still had hoped that he would return to work someday. He thought he could work at the campgrounds, mowing the lawn and doing maintenance work. As much as I didn't think he would ever work again, I didn't dare tell him. We all need to have hope. If he had returned to work, his access to the free formula for his tube would have been cut off. He needed that formula, a very expensive formula, and all of us worked too hard to get that for him. Besides, with my father's condition the way that it had been, I can't imagine how he ever could have worked – the formula is almost a moot point.

No, Mom and I had no idea Dad was close to death. Dad had been sick before I was born. Twenty-nine years to be exact. There were times throughout those twenty-nine years that no one believed he would live as long as he did. Doctors, who treated him years ago, were surprised to treat him again, believing he might have died years before. They didn't understand how resilient Dad was. He always pulled through until the one day he didn't.

∞

The last summer before Dad passed away was one of the best summers Dad had in a while. He went camping and went for drives with Mom. He babysat Ben and Hallie on multiple occasions for short periods of time. Physically, he was getting stronger, and we were all adjusting to a life that didn't involve hospitals. He was enjoying his life, and we were enjoying having Dad at home.

He was even starting to drive. After his license had expired in March that year, he didn't immediately renew it, and we weren't sure if they would let him. Dad was determined he was getting his license, each and every time it would expire.

"What's the worst that's going to happen?" Mom said after he went to get his new license that year. "They just won't give it to him."

Neither one of us were brave enough to go in with him. As we waited for Dad to come out, doubts set in. They probably wouldn't give him his license, and he would be utterly disappointed, we figured.

However, twenty-five minutes later, he came out. Not only did he get his class five license to drive a regular car, but he also had his class three license until November of that year. He could only keep his class three license to operate any truck over 14,000 kg or combination, including special equipment or a gooseneck trailer, provided that he could get a doctor who would fill out his physical to meet their requirements.

"The next doctor's appointment I have, I'll get that filled out," he said, pointing to the form.

"I think you should just let it go," Mom told him, "and be grateful for the license you have."

∞

August 25th started as a good day for Dad. He got up early and made Mom breakfast: eggs, toast, and bacon. It was their thirty-first wedding anniversary the day before, but he hadn't been feeling well, so he wanted to make up for it and do something special for Mom before she went to work that day.

I started my four days off from work that morning and was planning on going mini-golfing with a client I work with privately. Dad had mentioned in the past, prior to that day, that he would like to go and I welcomed him to come with us. Dad had a good relationship with the client I was working with, and the client really liked him.

He hummed and he hawed about it but, ultimately, decided he should visit his mother. Nena had started a new medication to help with her knee pain and was, unfortunately, experiencing a lot of pain. Dad was worried about her.

I dropped him off at the Health Centre to get Mom's keys. He went inside, talked to Mom for a few minutes, got the keys, and headed towards the side parking lot where the car was parked. Unfortunately, he fell on some uneven pavement.

Well, sadly, he broke his femur and dislocated his hip. He needed surgery. It was such a nasty fall that had the bone broke a few more inches above, he would have required a total hip replacement.

Luckily, he got along well with the surgery – well lucky in that he didn't die during the surgery. Unfortunately, however, the main complication that he experienced post-surgery was with his kidneys. See, his uncontrolled diabetes had led to chronic kidney disease prior to the surgery. The stress of both the fall and the surgery was a lot of pressure on his kidneys, and his body wasn't able to keep up with the demands. He started to retain a lot of fluid. His fingers and his hands were doubled in size. His feet were swollen like balloons. None of the medications seemed to work. He couldn't get rid of the fluid. His skin would get tight and itchy and he hated the way it made him look.

The pain was intense, but he had no choice but to manage it. He was afraid to do physio but he reluctantly agreed to work with the physiotherapist. After his surgery, the physiotherapist at the Queen Elizabeth Hospital in Charlottetown had given him some exercises to do in bed to keep his hip moving.

Dad did not want to do the exercises. Mom and I would beg and nag until he would get tired and eventually cave in and do some of the exercises. I can remember an instance when Dad was trying to avoid his exercises.

"It's a good time to do your exercises," Mom had suggested.

"I will later," Dad promised.

"Why don't you do it now and get it over with?" I had offered.

He mumbled something but eventually moved his feet and legs. He liked doing the exercises on his own and didn't want any help. Most of the time, Mom and I barely paid any attention as he did his exercises.

A few minutes later, after he had completed his exercises, he laid back down. "There, now don't ask me to do them again. I'm done for today."

"You did great, Dad," I said, "but can you do it on the broken hip side?"

"I was just trying to get the hang of the exercises," he claimed.

∞

Eventually, he was sent to Western Hospital to heal once again before he could go home. Before he fell, he had good and bad days with the nausea and vomiting. After he fell, he only seemed to have bad days.

"We're sending you to Prince County in Summerside," one doctor had told him during the morning rounds. More investigations were needed to see what was causing him to have so much nausea and vomiting.

"Maybe this is what I need to feel better," Dad told Mom and me after the doctor had left.

"Hey, Summerside is not that far away," I replied with an encouraging tone.

Mom and I both agreed Prince County was probably a better option for Dad. They had more doctors and professionals. There would be more access to equipment. Things would get done faster and he could come home sooner.

∞

Dad was admitted to the palliative/medical unit and placed in a palliative room. We were a little concerned by the choice of a palliative room. Palliative - the name alone is enough to give you chills. Our thoughts in regards to the name of the room were unpleasant and sad – thoughts of which that whoever was admitted typically never made it out alive. *Dad wasn't palliative*, we thought.

So, we had made plans to bring him home. Mom and I had discussed the changes we needed to make in the house so he wouldn't feel like a prisoner in his own home. We discussed ways to make the house safe and easy to exit with his broken hip if there was ever a fire. Because with our luck, we had to be prepared.

"Why is Trevor in a palliative room?" My mother had snapped at the nurse on the first day he was admitted to Prince County Hospital.

The nurse smiled, probably with empathy.

"Trevor has a lot of equipment and we needed to make sure there was plenty of room for us to work."

Mom sat down, satisfied with the answer. Just like we thought, he wasn't really in palliative care.

∞

On Thanksgiving Monday, Mom and I visited again. Amy and the kids also visited. We found him to be very quiet but still very capable of holding a conversation.

He still ate a bite of my sub. It was food that he wasn't supposed to eat but Mom, nor I, could ever say 'no' to one of his requests. For months, when Dad was in the hospital, he had intense cravings. Food was all he could think of and we couldn't deny him any of his requests.

We would shut his curtains and keep a close eye on any staff entering his room while he took a bite or two. He wouldn't eat a lot, just enough to satisfy his cravings. If he binged and ate more than a bite or two, he would usually get pretty sick.

"What did you think of Dad today?" I asked Mom on the way home from the hospital that day.

"They're giving him too much for pain," Mom replied. They changed his pain medication from intermittent needles to a continuous pump. "We want him to be comfortable but not that comfortable."

"We'll have to talk to someone about it," I told her.

When Monday came, neither Mom nor I could visit. We were both working. Nena visited Dad. She found that he was a little too drugged. She was about to talk to a nurse or a doctor, but Dad told her to mind her own business. For the first time since he fell, the pain wasn't that bad.

∞

On Tuesday, I was off and it was my turn to get someone to find a balance between too much medication and not enough.

When I arrived at the hospital, there was a change. The Dad I always knew, who always mumbled something, regardless if he was happy or not, no longer greeted me. He was transformed into a state of consciousness difficult to describe. He responded with a 'yes' or a 'no' to questions but nothing else. He only glanced at me when I called him by name. The sparkle was gone from his eyes. It was very strange, sad and maybe a little scary but certainly, disconcerting.

"Dad?" I said, taking him by the hand. His hand was cold, colder than I had ever felt it before. "What's wrong?"

He didn't respond.

"What is going on?" I asked the nurse and the doctor who came to examine him. "Are these changes caused by the drugs?"

"I believe they are. We will cut back on the drugs and see if it makes a difference," the doctor promised. "I will send him for some tests. Is your mother coming down to visit today?"

"She can come," I responded.

Mom didn't take time off for Dad unless it was really important. Mom liked to work. It was her relief from what was happening with Dad. However, if something was happening, she wanted to be there. Plus, financially she needed to work. With Dad being sick for so many years, she couldn't just take off from work every time Dad was sick and good jobs were few and far between.

"He signed his own code a few weeks ago." The words made me panic. Why did he want to know? Were we at that point it was necessary for a doctor to discuss it? Was I missing something?

Dad and I talked about what our hypothetical last wishes for treatment many times. It was a debate of what medical treatment we both would want to be done if we ever needed it. Would we want chemo if the only purpose was to extend life a little longer? Are the side effects of medications really worth a few months more even if it couldn't heal you?

I knew he was a fighter, but I also wondered what he signed. A few weeks before at Western Hospital, Dad told Mom and me that he had signed his code. Mom later signed it without even looking at it. No one discussed what he chose. It would not happen anytime soon, we figured. It was one of those "just in case" type of forms.

I called Mom and told her she should take the afternoon off from work and come down. I was nervous and wanted Mom to take care of everything and make them fix Dad. I wanted her to ask the questions I was afraid to ask.

"I'll be there as soon as I can," she responded.

When Mom got there, things were settling down. We had to wait to see if there was going to be a difference in Dad's state of consciousness with the change in drug dosage. The doctor had asked no other questions, and we weren't as concerned.

I went home about supper time. Mom left later. She asked if Dad wanted her to stay, but he shook his head to say 'no'.

∞

On Wednesday as I left again to see Dad, we hoped for a better visit. Mom was getting ready to go to work.

"I'll see you tonight," I told her.

When I arrived at the hospital, things were even more intense than the day before. The nurses were even more concerned than they had been the day before. The doctor was paying more visits that morning and Dad was no longer responding to yes or no questions. Only once did he respond to "Dad" with a small glance.

"Is your Mom coming to visit your Dad today?" The doctor responded.

Again, I answered, "She can,' I paused, "Should I ask her to come?"

Usually, the arrangement we had was that if someone was visiting Dad, especially in Summerside, Mom would visit on her days off.

"I don't need her to come yet," he replied, "Would your family be okay if we had to send him to Halifax?"

I nodded in agreement. Since he had fallen, I believed Dad would eventually wind up back in Halifax. It was even easier to travel to Halifax, Landon and Amy were living there.

"What about surgery?" he asked. "Do you think he would want to have any more surgeries?"

I nodded to say 'yes', wondering if this guy read Dad's medical file at all. Dad had multiple surgeries in the past few years. He always came through surgeries like a trooper. What was one more surgery, if he needed it?

"Are we still thinking these changes are related to too many drugs?" I asked.

"It could be," the nurse responded honestly. "He is a puzzle that we need to solve."

"We've stopped the drugs completely," the doctor answered.

Stopping the pain medication completely was probably one of Dad's biggest fears. Dad hated to be in pain. Generally, people don't like pain but Dad hated it.

"Mom," I said when I called her at work. "Please don't rush from work but you should take the afternoon off again and come when you can."

"Okay," she responded.

I held Dad's hand, trying to warm him up.

"My brother's in Ontario, doing a course. It would be a little difficult, but he can come home. Should he come home?" I blurted out when the nurse and doctor returned.

I wondered if I sounded stupid. I was worried but were we at the point where we really had to worry? Dad's health was always a concern for my entire life.

Landon just couldn't come home every time that Dad had a hiccup.

"Not right now," the doctor assured me before leaving the room, "but we'll keep a close eye on him."

"I think we will change his position in bed to help his breathing," the nurse stated. I wasn't sure if raising the bed was what Dad would have wanted. Since he had broken his hip, Dad did not like sitting up in bed. He claimed it hurt too much, but I didn't care about his pain in those moments. That is to say that his ability to breathe was a much higher priority.

It appeared the moment that his bed was raised, there was a significant change in his breathing pattern. His breathing was more labored and it sounded like he was struggling.

"I'm calling the respiratory therapist," the nurse announced. The stress was evident in her tone.

I called Landon.

"Let me talk to him," Landon begged after I told him about what had happened that day.

I put the phone on speaker and placed it near Dad.

"Is that him breathing?"

"Yes," I answered.

"He doesn't sound good. Should I come home?"

It's always a tough decision to decide if someone else should come home, especially when it concerned Dad. Nobody wants to be the one to tell another person, especially family, 'no don't come home yet', because in a case like that one, something could happen. It was Dad. He always pulled through.

"Some people get really sick to their stomach when they see someone being suctioned. Would you like to step out for a moment?" The nurse asked.

"No," I responded, "I'd like to stay if I can."

Years of visiting Dad in the hospital prepared me to know what should happen when someone would be suctioned. As prepared as I thought I was, I wasn't. Vomit came up, spilling content all over his Johnny shirt.

"This man needs to be intubated. He aspirated," the respiratory therapist said.

The respiratory therapist looked at me.

"He is a very sick man. Do you want to put him through that?"

I panicked, naturally. Never had I had to make a decision so huge before, but I knew the answer.

"Yes."

The doctor who I had been talking to earlier that day had come back in. Again, I was asked if we wanted to continue with the invasive treatment.

"I know you don't know Dad, but he is a fighter. I want to keep fighting," I murmured, struggling to find my words.

"I understand. He has a full code anyways." the doctor stated.

Plans were being made rapidly to move Dad to the ICU.

I called Mom.

"You need to come now!" I spoke with urgency.

"I'm leaving right now," she promised.

I called Landon.

"Things have changed. You need to come home."

"Okay," he responded, "I'll make the plans."

I called Nena.

"You need to come to the hospital."

"What's going on?" She asked.

A nurse gently tapped me.

"You need to come with us. The doors to the ICU will be locked if you don't come now."

"Atara!" my grandmother said into the phone.

"Nena," I said, probably sounding harsh. "You need to come." I hung up.

"We'll find you a waiting room," the nurse suggested, "while we get him ready."

By this time, my courage was failing. I was crying. I wished it was a nightmare and that I would wake up. I was alone, inside the little waiting room. I wasn't sure when anyone would arrive or when I could see Dad.

Inside the ICU waiting room, I was joined by Amy's Mom. She was the head of the department there. Amy, very kindly, had called her so I would not have to be alone.

"Is there anything I can do?" Cathy asked me.

What does one request when their father is dying? A stat of an order of Lorazepam? Doctors as talented as the actors that played hotshot doctors on TV? I wanted someone who could rush in, find a solution using some new technology never heard of before or perform a risky surgery that could save him.

Instead, I asked that a priest could come in and anoint him with the oils of the sick.

∞

When the priest arrived, I could see Dad for the first time since he had been moved to the ICU. Dad had his own nurse and I was thankful that Amy's mother was near me because don't we all work a little harder when the boss is around? I wanted everyone on staff to work as hard as they possibly could for him.

I held his hand. It was cold and wet. He was swollen so much that the fluid was seeping through his skin.

The priest prayed and anointed him. God had forgiven Dad for every sin he had committed.

I asked a nurse for a towel. The fluid seeping from his skin was making his body cold and Dad minded the cold even at the best of times. He often joked that Canada was the wrong spot for him to live. He needed to live in California.

I held his hand and I talked to him. I don't remember what I was telling him but I wanted him to know he was not alone. I tried my hardest to keep talking, even when I had run out of things to tell him.

Finally, I heard Mom and Leah coming in. I felt like a little girl again. I wanted Mom to tell me things would be okay but she couldn't. Nena came in a little later.

The staff asked if we could leave and go back to the waiting room. They had to do more work on him that was harder to do with the influx of people. They also wanted to change his sheets that were now drenched with the fluid draining from his body.

∞

While we were in the waiting room, a surgeon that was treating Dad came in to discuss the case with us. He spoke about Dad's health and how much he had already gone through. He spoke about how our bodies resist machines like a feeding tube and medical procedures after a certain amount of time. It wasn't natural to live the way Dad did.

He spoke about our desire to continue with life support. He wanted us to think about some questions that he was going to ask but he didn't require a response. How fair was it to put Dad through all of it? He spoke about Dad's already poor quality of life and what it would be like after all of the trauma if he were to survive.

I started to answer but the doctor stopped me, reminding me that he did not want answers. The doctor's questions were making me furious. He didn't know Dad. Dad made the best of the situation he was in every time. He complained sometimes about pain but he never really complained that he was sick or all the things he was missing out on in life. He never complained that he wasn't able to do the things that he once loved. Never did I hear Dad ask, "Why is this happening to me?"

"My husband is a fighter," Mom said, "I understand what you're telling me but I promised him many times that we would never give up on him. I have to respect his wishes. I can't let him go without a fight."

The doctor wished us the best and said he was leaving the country for the weekend. I was happy because he didn't seem to really believe in Dad's ability to fight and I didn't want him and his negativity around Dad - even if he was just trying to do his job.

Another doctor was more hopeful. He had treated Dad a few times in the past and we always had faith in him. He spoke about all of Dad's health issues. He listened attentively when Mom explained how important it was for us to continue to fight. He respected our decision and had a very calming nature. He believed that we would not have to decide to stop fighting. Dad would tell us if he could beat this or not, in his own way. We just had to listen.

He believed Dad had about a 50/50 chance. In my mind, a 50/50 chance for Dad was actually more 60/40 in Dad's favor because of his determination and strength. It wasn't the first time he wasn't expected to make the night and we had reason to hope he could do it again.

As time progressed that evening, the nurse was concerned with his vitals. She noticed a change. Still, we continued to hope that things would turn around, and if they couldn't, we hoped that Dad would at least wait until Landon could be there.

∞

Landon and Amy arrived at 11:00 pm. Landon was exhausted from his course and the day's events. He was battling a cold and terrified that he would pass Dad another infection on top of it. We later found out that Landon was suffering from viral meningitis. He was admitted a few days later to the hospital.

"Dad, I hope you know this is not a free pass for you to die. I did not come home to watch you die," Landon said, angrily. "You have to fight harder."

Dad moved his fingers. It was the most we had gotten, as far as movement went, all night.

"Open your eyes, Dad," Landon begged. He probably wanted to sound firm but it came out as more of a plea. It didn't matter that Dad was medicated and couldn't wake up. Landon wanted his miracle. We all wanted it.

"I'll help you, Dad," Landon said, as he gently opened Dad's eyelids.

Dad's blue eyes were focused. They did not roam around the room. His pupils did not hide. They remained focused on us as if he knew what was going on.

"Landon, you need to close his eyes," Amy said. "They'll dry out."

Landon gently closed his eyes, not wanting to cause Dad any more pain.

"Come on Dad," he pleaded again. "You can do this. I know you can. When you get better, you and I will go to the car dealership. Any car you want, you got it."

We looked at Landon, but he continued talking to Dad.

"If you want a truck, you can get a truck. You can have my truck if you want it. Can you move your fingers again?"

It looked like they moved a bit but it could have been our imagination hoping and wanting Dad's fingers to move.

"Landon?" Amy said cautiously, not wanting to upset him. "You shouldn't ask your Dad to move his fingers. He needs all his energy to fight. You're asking him to do too much."

"Okay," Landon agreed, "Dad, you don't have to move your fingers, but when you get better, you and I will get the parts to fix your motorcycle. If you don't want to work on it, we'll find someone to do it for you."

Landon stayed quiet. We stared at the monitors, not fully aware of how they worked. Landon and I were both hoping for the same thing, Mom would tell us that everything was going to be okay and we would watch as Dad started to recover. We hoped we would see a sudden jump on the screen and that Dad was going to have a miraculous recovery. We wanted this nightmare to be a story we would tell in a few years' time about another time that Dad defied the odds.

Dad's bed had to be changed again. He was soaking wet. He was still seeping so much fluid through his skin because of the swelling.

We were asked to step into the waiting room while they cleaned Dad up.

Mom stood in the hallway, staring at the pictures.

"Do they save anyone here?"

She pointed to the plaques under some of the pictures.

"They are all in memory. It's not much encouragement."

"Let's go wait with Landon and Amy in the waiting room," I suggested.

∞

"Do you think you should tell your Dad it's okay if he has to let go?" Amy suggested, treading carefully with a polite tone.

"No," Landon said, "that's not going to happen. Dad is 53-years-old. It's not okay for him to give up. It's not his time yet. We still need him."

Amy opened her mouth, but Landon stopped her.

"If your Dad was sick, would you be okay with telling him that he could give up?"

She didn't respond. She knew better than to say anything else. He didn't want to hear it. Landon just wasn't ready.

The nurse came to the waiting room.

"You can go back in but it could be a long night. Why don't some of you try to get some sleep?"

No one wanted to rest. No one wanted to be far away from Dad when they didn't have to be, but if Dad was still holding on, it could be a long waiting game. We would need our strength. We decided to split into two. Landon and Mom would sleep first. Landon looked exhausted, and Mom looked equally as exhausted.

Amy and I sat with Dad. My eyes remained glued to the monitor. My hands trying to desperately warm his hands.

"Look, Amy," I said, pointing to the monitor, "that's the highest blood pressure that I have seen all night."

She looked at the monitor and nodded in agreement. His last few blood pressures were getting higher. His systolic reading would raise but his diastolic reading would lower. The next reading might raise the diastolic number but lower the systolic reading.

"We just need time," I rambled. "We just need enough time for his antibiotics to kick in so he has a good chance."

"Your Dad is strong," Amy said. "He might overcome this."

"God, please just give us time," I prayed out loud.

We sat for two hours, silently. I prayed to God, begging him to grant my prayers and let Dad live. I made every bargain possible as I stared at the monitors, hoping for an increase in his numbers.

"I am going to go to my parents' house," Amy said finally. "The kids will wake up soon and my parents will have to go to work."

Amy went to the room where Landon and Mom were sleeping, or rather *trying to* sleep unsuccessfully. Mom came back to Dad's room.

"Atara, you need to go to the waiting room and try to fall asleep. I know it's hard, but we don't know how long this will last and we will all need our strength and I would like to have some alone time with your father," she said.

I nodded in agreement and left her alone with Dad. I wondered what she was going to tell him. Was Mom going to beg him to fight? If anyone could make Dad do something, it was Mom. She demanded little from him so when she did he felt like he had to try his hardest. I also wondered if talking to Dad was making a difference. Could he hear us?

∞

"Do you think that Dad will pull through?" Landon asked when we were alone.

"I really hope so," I replied.

"Put a status on social media and ask people to pray for him. Dad needs all the prayers he can get right now."

It was a good idea. The status was barely posted when Mom came into the waiting room.

"The nurse is noticing a change and she thinks that maybe you guys should come back in if you want to be there in case something happens."

Quickly, I got up to go to the room. I made another silent plea to God to please spare him. I still needed him more than I thought God did.

The nurse took some blood from an inserted line.

"I have to call the doctor if you still want to continue treatment," she said. "I have depleted all the medications that were ordered. There's nothing else I can give him."

"Is he in pain?" Mom asked.

The nurse looked at Dad.

"I think he is somewhat comfortable but don't kid yourself, he is in some pain."

She had spoken several times throughout the evening about Dad's code. He was still a full code and we were still unwilling to change it. She reminded us that if Dad's heart was to stop beating, with his current code, they would need to do full CPR to revive him.

"Guys?" Mom said, looking at both Landon and me after the nurse had left the room, "I'm not giving up on your father, but I'm not sure how much longer we can continue. I don't know if I can see them doing compressions on your father's chest. He is so small. They'll break his ribs."

"Do whatever you want, Mom," Landon mumbled, "I'll support whatever decision you make."

"We will see what the bloodwork says," Mom said, solemnly.

The bloodwork came back.

"It's not good," the nurse stated. "His system is shutting down. He is in multi-organ failure. The only thing right now that is keeping him alive is the medication that is raising his blood pressure."

I stared at the nurse and though I didn't know her, I hated her. While she was only doing her job, I couldn't help but blame her. Why couldn't she have come into the room with news that I wanted to hear? I only wanted to hear that Dad was getting better. For the rest of my life, as polite and professional as she was, she was going to be the person that I would associate the worst moment of my life with.

He called Nena. We didn't really want Nena to come down by herself, but we needed to tell her what was going on. She refused to say goodbye to Dad on the phone just like she had done every time before when Dad had called before a surgery to say his goodbyes to her. She wanted to keep her hope that something was going to change.

Landon called Leah next. He asked her to come down. Mom needed her big sister, more than ever before. It was difficult for Leah. She lost her husband in the same hospital, less than two years ago. She wasn't sure that she could see someone else that she loved die there but, regardless, she agreed to come.

∞

"We have a decision to make," Mom said, "it has to be unanimous."

"Mom, if we ever got our miracle and Dad lived long enough to wake up, I couldn't take it knowing he could still die. They'll never give him any transplants. Can you imagine how Dad would feel if he knew he was going to die? He can't come back from this. We have to let him go," I said, as I struggled to speak. My throat was closing over.

"Landon?" Mom said. "What do you think?"

"It's whatever you think, Mom," Landon said again.

"I don't want them doing compressions," Mom stated. "I can't watch your father go through that. They'll break his chest."

When the nurse came back in, Mom said, "I think we made our decision, but I would like to wait until my sister gets here."

It seemed like the longest hour waiting for Leah to get there. When she got there, we filled her in on everything that had happened since she had left.

"Make sure we didn't miss anything," Mom instructed Leah.

Leah talked to the nurse. She looked at the monitors.

"Lorna, nothing was missed. Nothing else can be done for him."

"Then I want to stop his treatment," Mom said. "I'm going to tell the nurse."

As she got up, Dad raised his arm like he was waving. The same way he did most times when we left his hospital room. Some say it was probably a muscle reflex, but it had meaning for me. It was his permission to let him go. It was his way of saying goodbye. Mom left the room and went to speak to the nurse.

The nurse came into the room. We had to leave while she turned off the monitors and took out the equipment that was keeping him alive.

A few minutes later, when we could go in the room, things were different. The monitor, that I had spent all night watching, was black. Dad was breathing only by mouth, no tube was inserted. He wasn't struggling for breath. He looked like he was comfortable, the most comfortable that I had seen him in the past twenty-four hours.

"We love you Dad," I said as I reached to hold his hand.

"I'm proud of you, Dad," Landon told him. "I'll make sure that we are all okay. You don't have to worry about any of us anymore."

"I love you, Trevor," Mom said, as she held his other hand. "I'll see you again someday."

It took less than ten minutes for Dad to pass away. He didn't struggle. It wasn't hard to watch like you may imagine. It was devastatingly sad and it hurt but it wasn't hard to watch. Maybe because it appeared almost as if he had just forgotten to breathe.

The four of us walked out of the hospital together. I watched as tears fell from Mom's eyes. We had spent so much time in that hospital, and the other hospitals, and now that part of our life would be over. No longer would we have to sit in uncomfortable chairs and search for things to talk about because we had discussed everything already or choose through food in hospital cafeterias or vending machines because we had spent our entire day at the hospital. We wouldn't have to make plans about how we were going to work and make sure that Dad had enough visitors. The turmoil of hoping and praying that Dad was going to get better was over. It was very strange.

Instead, we had a new turmoil to deal with. We couldn't wish him back. It wouldn't be fair. His body went through too much. He had lived a life where he loved many and was loved very much in return. Dad had good memories, bad memories and a lot of suffering. His suffering was over, but now it was our turn to be in pain.

Grief can be a selfish process if you believe in God. It is still a necessary part of the process of surviving a loss. I believe Dad is in a better place where he is no longer hindered by tube feedings and medications. His body movements are once again youthful and I imagine he has a big goofy grin on his face. He is near God who is glad to have him home.

∞

It's difficult to get over grief. I'm not sure if a person ever does. I think you eventually find a new normal in your life - a new way to live. It's not the same life as it was before nor would I really want it to be the same. It can't be. A part of our family is missing. We have to continue to live without this person who, along with Mom, started our family.

We won't forget him. It's impossible to forget someone who gave us so much to remember. Someday, if I'm ever lucky enough to have children, they will know all about their grandfather. I'll tell them all about the man who could roll his tongue and tell a great story. I'll tell them the story about how he invited a complete stranger into our home without warning. My children will know all about their grandfather who made me break the rules and bring him meat sticks, sandwiches and pop when he wasn't supposed to have it. I know as long as I live a part of Dad will live on.

Epilogue

"Live life for the moment because everything else is uncertain."

Louis Tomlinson

One night, not long after Dad had passed away, I asked Mom in conversation, "Did you ever think about leaving Dad?" You guys didn't really have the kind of life you probably expected when you got married."

Mom and Dad had a good relationship. They didn't fight often and it never lasted long when they did but it wasn't an easy life.

It took a strong person to endure what Mom did. When Dad was sick, she managed to care for two kids, work her full-time job, and care for Dad. She didn't live the life she deserved. She wasn't able to go on trips or pamper herself at the salon. Sometimes she had to use the hair dye from a box because she couldn't always afford to get it done professionally and her scalp would burn for days after.

Yet, not once did I ever hear her complain. She never envied her friends or what they had. She was content with what she had and the life she lived.

Mom thought about the question I asked, "The day I married your father, we made a vow to God to love each other in sickness and in health, through the good and the bad."

"So," I said, "you really only stayed with Dad because you made a promise to God?" I was hoping she was going to give a different response. I wanted to believe my parents' marriage of over thirty years was based on more than a promise.

"No," she stated, "that is not why I stayed with your father. The day I married your father was the day that I stopped being Lorna Perry. I became a part of a team with your father. It was us against anything. We became a WE instead of a me and a him."

She took her time to reflect before she spoke again, "When your father got hurt that day, it didn't just happen to him. It also happened to me. I just couldn't feel his physical pain."

She stared at me for a moment, "When I married your father, we hoped things would have turned out differently. It wasn't supposed to be like this," she continued. "Your father was working at Papa's garage with the hope that it would be his someday. I was working at the hospital. Your father hoped that I would be able to quit and work part-time at the shop and stay at home with the four children we planned on having."

"But Dad got hurt," I said, "and nothing turned out like it was supposed to."

She nodded in agreement, "Life is so unpredictable. Anything can happen and you, of all people, know that." With a deep breath, she added, "You have to find that person who is going to be beside you for all the bumps and hurdles that life throws at you."

I listened, caught up in her words, as she continued, "I wanted your father by my side. I wouldn't have wanted an easy life if it wouldn't have involved your father."

Dad is gone now. It's difficult to write the sentence and believe it. With as many chances as Dad had with his health, I really believed Dad would outlive us all.

Mom is strong, stronger than I expected her to be. Not a day goes by where Dad's name is not mentioned. Sometimes it is with a chuckle and there are other days that she struggles with memories of Dad and hopes and wishes for what could have been.

When I think about Dad and his journey through life, I think about the critical moments. Moments that when you're older and you look back on life, you remember that as the moment that marked the change. The moment that nothing would ever be the same again.

When I consider those critical moments, I think about the decisions that led to that moment. That one moment that may have been changed by a single decision made years before, maybe in the heat of the moment or without a second thought.

I've come to the conclusion that some of our choices are the forks in the road. Sometimes the direction we will choose is obvious but other times we struggle with what direction we should choose. When we do start our path, we are never really sure where it will lead to exactly. Most of us would like to believe that the road we choose is going to be wonderful with a smooth surface and beautiful scenery. Sometimes the road we end up on has rough patches along the way and you wonder if you'll ever get through it.

If Dad had chosen to stay home the day he had gotten hurt or had even gone to lunch earlier, he might not have gotten hurt that day. Maybe a different outcome would have resulted if Dad had chosen to go to a different hospital following the accident. Had we found the money to send him to a top neurosurgeon, he may have recovered better.

Had I been able to convince Dad on August 25th, 2016 to come mini-golfing with me instead of picking up Mom's car, he may not have fallen. If he had not fallen and broken his hip, he might still be alive today.

Mom and Dad anticipated when they married that they were going to grow old together. Unfortunately, that didn't happen.

Mom could choose to complain that life is not fair. She would have every reason to do so. She wasn't a bad person. She went to church and prayed to God. She helped people when she could.

She could wish that Trevor had never went to work that morning of the accident but had they not gone down that road, who knows what could have been waiting for them on the other road? The garage could have plummeted and they might have gone bankrupt. They may have waited until a better time to have another kid and I wouldn't have been born (which would have been the real tragedy). Had we not developed a close family bond, Landon or I could have developed a strong drug addiction and died from our addiction at a young age. We don't know what was waiting down the other road. It could have been much worse.

ACKNOWLEDGEMENTS

There are so many people to thank that I could write an acknowledgement just as a sequel. This is the short and sweet version.

First and foremost, I want to thank Mom, Landon, Amy and their children. Thank you for giving me permission to tell our journey. I couldn't imagine going through life with any other family by my side. I love you all.

To my extended family: Thanks for always having our backs. You all mean so much to us.

I'd also like to thank any doctors who ever treated and consulted in Dad's care. A big thank you also goes to the compassionate and empathetic nurses who cared for Dad. There're too many names to name but you know who you are. Special thanks go to all other hospital staff who treated Dad with respect and dignity. Your kindness will never be forgotten by my family.

Thank you to all who helped my family. Your prayers and acts of kindness gave us the strength to continue on our road. Special thanks go to an extraordinary person who went above and beyond to help our family and is a ***berry berry nice person.***

Thank you to all clergy and the M.J. Rooney Council Knights of Columbus for your many visits. Dad drew comfort from your prayers.

Finally, a thank you to you, the reader. As many words as I claim to know, I don't know enough to express my gratitude to all of you. I hope you enjoyed reading about the Yuill's journey and the roads we ended up on.

85176930R00152

Made in the USA
Columbia, SC
31 December 2017